The Reward of Doing

The
REWARD
of DOING

JOHN COLLOPY

Advantage | Books

Published by Advantage, Charleston, South Carolina.
Member of Advantage Media.

ADVANTAGE is a registered trademark, and the Advantage colophon is a trademark of Advantage Media Group, Inc.

Printed in the United States of America.

10 9 8 7 6 5 4 3 2 1

ISBN: 978-1-64225-795-3 (Paperback)
ISBN: 978-1-64225-794-6 (eBook)

LCCN: 2022923885

Cover design by Matthew Morse.
Layout design by Matthew Morse.

This publication is designed to provide accurate and authoritative information in regard to the subject matter covered. It is sold with the understanding that the publisher is not engaged in rendering legal, accounting, or other professional services. If legal advice or other expert assistance is required, the services of a competent professional person should be sought.

Advantage Media helps busy entrepreneurs, CEOs, and leaders write and publish a book to grow their business and become the authority in their field. Advantage authors comprise an exclusive community of industry professionals, idea-makers, and thought leaders. Do you have a book idea or manuscript for consideration? We would love to hear from you at **AdvantageMedia.com**.

CONTENTS

INTRODUCTION

Why is it so easy for us to identify what we want, yet seemingly so hard to take the steps we need to get it?

That mystifies me and always has. I've encountered this phenomenon more times than I can count, as I've watched people with achievable dreams and a route to making them come true fail to follow through. Smart people, most of them, with realistic, realizable goals. Yet when it comes to changing their behavior in the ways they must to get where they want to go, they *just don't do it*.

Why is that?

I've coached thousands of people at all levels of accomplishment to greater success in their lives and work. As an Alcoholics Anonymous (AA) member and recovering alcoholic, I've mentored many people working toward getting and staying sober and heard all kinds of stories

over cups of coffee. I built a thriving real estate business from the ground up, RE/MAX Results, with sales over $9.5 billion a year. I like to think that thanks to all I've done and seen and been, I've acquired a fair understanding of human nature and what makes us tick. But I still can't wrap my mind around why it is that people's actions so rarely align with what they say they want to accomplish.

Maybe your substance abuse issues have made you homeless, and one cold, wet night you think, "Man, I wish I had an apartment." Well, you *could* get an apartment, but you'd have to quit drinking and getting high. But you don't want to quit. You like it. Okay, then— you just made a choice that defines what you really want. You don't really want a place to live because you like drinking more. That's one example of what I mean. Granted, most of us don't come to this point, but there are so many areas in our life that are like that—choices we make by default because we can't or won't or aren't willing to make our actions conform to what we say we want.

The fact is all those old bromides we were raised on are true; our happiness in life is 100 percent up to us. Our choices dictate our outcomes. The conundrum is why we so consistently make the wrong ones.

OUR HAPPINESS IN LIFE IS 100 PERCENT UP TO US.

To be honest, I've never been good at taking advice. When I got sober, I wanted to succeed at staying that way. When my counselor told me I'd have to change my behavior and stop hanging out at the bar with my friends because they were all drug users and drunks, I protested. These were my pals, guys I'd known my whole life!

My sobriety counselor, a former Catholic priest, just shook his head. "You can't do that, John."

I'd always had a problem with authority, and I'd had twelve years of Catholic school, so naturally this was all it took to make me decide, "That's exactly what I'm going to do."

So when I got out of treatment, I went down to the bar I used to hang out at and drank Cokes with my buddies. To be honest, it wasn't as much fun as I'd thought it would be. The best part was that I made some money shooting pool, because I was the only sober guy in there at eleven o'clock at night. But watching other people get drunk just wasn't doing it for me, and finally, after a few weeks of it, I decided, "This sucks. I'm not going back there. I'm going to order a pizza and stay home." That's what I did, and I liked it—and I didn't see my friends for years. The counselor was right, in terms of my happiness and mental health. I just didn't like being told my sobriety hinged on it because I'm naturally contrary.

Later, when my sobriety was rock solid and I was getting happier with who I was and more comfortable in my new skin, I started picking times that I could see my friends, making the rules about how that would go. Whether that meant we went to a Vikings game together or had lunch at a favorite restaurant, I chose things we could do together that related to how I lived my new sober life. If I got invited to one of their houses for some wild party, I didn't go. My counselor was right again, but I had to do it my way.

Now I'm the guy who gives advice—on business plans, on jump-starting careers, on sobriety. Some of it comes free. Some of it people pay for, but even the ones who pay often disregard the advice. They fail to take the steps they need to take to get the outcome they claim to want. And this has led me to a conclusion I want to share with you.

All these people who won't do what they know they need to do to make their dreams come true? They're lying. To me, to themselves, to their partners; they don't want to achieve their dreams. They don't want to be happy. They don't want to succeed. I can't tell you why, but I can tell you that's the case.

Say you're a real estate sales executive, and you want to get better at it, so you come to see me for coaching. We meet every two weeks. You come into my office, and the first things I ask you are, "How many new contacts did you make since we met last? How many appointments did you go out on?" Depending on the answers you give me, I can predict with near-perfect certainty how many houses you're going to sell, because if you're going to sell houses, you've got to make contacts and go out on appointments. Period. No mystery, no tricks, just do the legwork. This often leads my mentees to ask, "You mean I have to make two hundred calls in two weeks?" Well, you might get lucky; the first two people you talk to might both want to buy houses, but that doesn't usually happen. That's why you have to make those two hundred calls and accurately track your activity level—to determine whether you're on track to achieve what you've verbalized to me as your goal.

This applies to personal life as well as business life. If you tell me you want to be in a happy marriage, but you and your partner are struggling to get along, the first thing I'll probably ask is whether you're seeing a therapist. Are the two of you meeting with a counselor? If the answer is no, then the question is, "What are you willing to change to achieve your goal of a happy marriage?" Clearly, you and your spouse have work to do, both as individuals and as a couple, if you're going to make it, because it's not going to get better until you get better. People have all kinds of excuses for not doing these things, but the fact is they're okay with being unhappy if it saves them from making the effort. And that is a choice.

Maybe you want to retire by the time you hit fifty. Clearly, the first thing you need to do is figure out how much money you're going to need to save to make that feasible. What kind of lifestyle do you want to have? How long can you reasonably expect to live? Most people who articulate the desire to retire at fifty begin with these questions and give up, stymied by doing the basic groundwork of planning.

Here's the thing. Whether we're talking about selling houses, or staying sober, or making your marriage work or your retirement dreams come true, you've got to admit that if you're not willing to take the steps that any of these things require, you don't really want them. You may think you do; maybe you feel like you should want them. But that's not the same thing. So what are you going to do to make your stated dreams square up to the reality of your efforts?

That's what this book is about and who it's for—people with dreams and goals that they somehow haven't managed to achieve. If that's you—if you're struggling to get your goals aligned with your efforts—this book is here to help you. My view is that happiness can be achieved if people stop getting in their own way and start doing what they say they want to do. This book is for everyone who wants to do better and be happier.

I've seen people do it, simply by getting clear on some fundamental ideas and applying them to their lives and choices.

In the chapters that follow, I'll dig into those ideas and help you see how they apply to you and your situation. Use them as tools to reframe your thinking, and you'll have a fighting chance to find the success that's eluded you up until now.

CHAPTER ONE

What You Say versus What You Do

Lucy was a bright, enthusiastic young woman who'd come to my office to ask for career advice. "I want to make a fortune selling real estate," she said. She had two children at home who she needed to support and was determined to succeed. She was ready and willing to put in the hard work. Where should she start?

But when I asked her to describe her day care plan, she admitted that she didn't really have one. She was sure that she didn't want to leave them in a day care center, though, because they were just too young.

I had to say, "Well, why don't you just stay home with the kids for three more years and come sell houses after they're able to go to day care?" Why did I suggest that? Because it was the only choice available for her at that point, given her determination not to leave her kids.

This is the kind of thing that makes me crazy—when people have an emotional investment in a stated desire but no plan to back it up. Lucy is a great person, bright and capable, but she lacked the infrastructure to allow her to move forward. If I'd told her to go ahead and get into real estate part time, she'd have become frustrated and frazzled by the competing demands on her time, and her chances of success would have been next to zero. Like I said, she's bright—so why couldn't she figure this out for herself?

I walk into all kinds of meetings with people who are adrenalized by a goal but are unable or unwilling to make the kinds of commitments and behavior changes necessary to achieve what they say they want. I've had literally thousands of conversations with would-be go-getters who were eager for a career with my company RE/MAX Results, one of the largest and most successful real estate franchises in the country. They give great pitches about how they can help us grow even bigger by fulfilling their dreams of working as agents with us. I've got over a thousand agents on board already, and I coach them to achieve the results they want, in both formal settings and casual conversations. They're all trying hard to achieve what Lucy wants— successful careers that make them wealthy. But so often they don't see or won't acknowledge that they're not taking the steps toward actually *doing* what they say they want to do. The consistency in what people espouse as opposed to what they accomplish is all too typical.

Where Does Taking Control over What You Say and What You Do Begin?

What so many of these people lack is the ability to see what it is that they really want, rather than what they say they want. That disconnect is what feeds their failure to make the commitments and behavior changes necessary to achieve their stated goal.

> *Happiness is when what you think, what you say, and what you do are in harmony.*
>
> **—MAHATMA GANDHI**

For Lucy, the tension was between her goals and her sense of responsibility to her kids. When she stopped to think about it, those kids were always going to come ahead of anything else she wanted, because the thing she wanted *most* was to be a good mother. Nothing wrong with that. It's a noble calling, and the world would probably be a better place if more parents looked at it that way. But that responsibility as she saw it couldn't coexist with the level of commitment her career goal required, so something had to give—and for a while at least, getting rich would have to wait.

What Holds You Back?

In my own experience, and what I've observed in other people like Lucy, the thing that holds most of them back is this: they don't know what they really want, and the things they *believe* they want are often in conflict with the things they *actually* want, so these competing wants struggle inside of them and undermine their ability to take the needed actions. They're not being honest with themselves, so there's no internal accord, and they can't move forward.

A lot of this is planted in us as kids, by how we're raised and what we see around us. Those early impressions often define our path. I grew up in a dysfunctional family. My mom and dad loved us. My dad was a devout Catholic; as long as he was alive, if he wasn't in the hospital, he went to church on Sunday. But every Wednesday, Friday, and Saturday night, he went out and got drunk with my mom. A third of the time they'd get in a fight, arguing and being stupid. And maybe five or six times a year, it would go to the next level of violence. I can tell you that when you're a kid living in the bedroom next to your parents' bedroom and your dad's beating up your mom, that's kind of rough. I hated my dad for being violent and chemically dependent. I wanted to be nothing like him.

Predictably, by the time I was thirteen, I was violent and an alcoholic. I wasn't a stupid kid, but it somehow failed to occur to me that if I didn't want to wind up like my dad, I probably shouldn't drink. I should maybe try harder in school, go to college, and get away from that life. But I didn't. I drank, and I loved it. A lot.

When I grew up and got sober, I was able to look up to bigger, more positive goals than just getting hammered and getting into gang fights. But as a kid and as a young adult, none of that was visible on my horizon, because I held on to the blue-collar attitude I was raised with—if you can make it to work on Monday, you don't have a drinking problem.

Even that low standard for behavior evaporated when I got injured and had to move back in with my family. All I did was drink. I had no other desire. My sole ambition was to somehow get to Southern California, become a bum, and stay high. That was my actual retirement plan, and I saw no fault in it. It didn't take long to hit bottom; my third DUI, driving without a license, and beating up the arresting officer landed me in jail.

My lawyer came to see me in lockup. "Let me tell you what's going to happen. Number one, you're going to jail. Number two, you're going into treatment. Number three, I'll keep you out of prison this time. Jail, treatment, no felony. Right? You want more than that? Go get a different lawyer."

I said, "I'll take it." I went to jail for a couple of months, I went to treatment, and then I got out and found a crappy minimum-wage job. But I stayed sober, and I liked it—and I got a promotion. Was it a miracle? Nope. I'd simply had enough.

I'd turned a corner and was doing things and making choices like someone who was done with self-sabotaging. Why? Because getting sober had taken off the blinders, and I could see not only where I'd been but where I could potentially go—assuming I made better choices (and identified better goals) than I had in the past.

What Does Success Look Like to You?

Lucy did as I suggested and came back when she felt safe leaving her kids in day care. And you know what? She became phenomenally successful, because she was able to put in the hours and effort required to build a meaningful career. She focused, she got her priorities in line, and she made good choices.

I don't want to suggest here that I've got some superpower that lets me spot who will succeed and who won't. It's a crapshoot, partly because life can take some surprising twists. But I can tell you that I see who does succeed—and it's those whose goals are in alignment with what they really want.

You have to decide what level of success for which you're willing to put in the work required to achieve—and you need to adjust your goals to reflect the reality of that willingness.

Take my fitness regimen—*please*. Three mornings a week, I get up much too early, go down to my home gym and do forty-five minutes of cardio on my treadmill. I don't enjoy it, but I do it. After that, my fitness coach comes over and puts me through my paces for another half hour. I tell her every time she's there how much I hate her. She just laughs and adds more reps. She knows I don't really hate her, but exercise is not my favorite activity.

So why do I do it? I do it because my genetics tell me I'm probably going to live to be old, and I decided some years back that I'd like to reach my old age with as much energy and physical agility and health as I can. My lifestyle is otherwise somewhat sedentary, and I don't want my legs to waste away because my butt is in a chair all the time. So I've made this accommodation between my natural urge to flop on the couch or sleep in and the amount of exercise I need to do to meet my goal. I've worked out a schedule that I can live with, and I stick to it because it's enough to do the job but not totally punishing. My coach is there to help me change it up and keep it from getting dull, and for added accountability.

KNOWING WHAT SUCCESS MEANS TO YOU IS CRITICAL TO GOAL SETTING AND ACHIEVEMENT.

Am I ripped? I am not. Would I like to have rock-hard pecs instead of man tits? Sure. I don't look the way I wish I did in the mirror. I know how it's done. If I want to have a more muscular chest, I'd have to work out four more times a week, adding on a new weightlifting program.

But the fact is I don't want to put in that much more work. It's not worth it to me. I have what I want; my health is good, I'm reasonably limber and strong, and my blood pressure's where it's supposed to be. Every now and then, I think to myself, "You ought to try and take it to the next level," but in my heart I know I don't really want to do the work. My goal was set appropriately for what I needed to achieve and how hard I was willing to work for it. I met it, and that feels good. For me, that's success.

Knowing what success means to you is critical to goal setting and achievement. Some people happily sail along pulling down $100,000 a year in sales and are delighted with that. Some people pull down a million bucks a year and whine about how hard their jobs are and why they can't make more. But the ones who combine financial success with happiness—who make money and love their lives—are those who are completely clear on what matters to them and are grounded by that. That frees them to succeed and allows them to enjoy the process.

How much money you make, how important your job is—that's irrelevant in the big scheme of things. Peace and serenity are where happiness comes from. If you're a dude living up in northern Minnesota, in a cabin, and all you do every day is feed the deer and pet your cat and dog, if that's what's cool for you, then that's as good as being the guy at the head of a Fortune 500 corporation for someone else. You don't have to be "something"; you have to be true to what you are. Everybody's unique, and everybody has a different flavor of what they want. As our lives change as we go along, even those change.

Some of the most successful newer members of the RE/MAX Results family are a bunch of young guys who all graduated from a local church-affiliated university. And they are kicking ass as Realtors; one of them, fresh out of college, pulled down $300,000 his first year. I never saw anybody succeed like that as a new agent. Now, he's still in his twenties and making about a million two. Not bad. Another guy from that same school is equally successful with his team. When

I met him, we talked for a little while, and he told me about himself. I couldn't help myself; I said to him, "You know you're a dork, right?"

He grinned back at me, clearly proud of it. "Yep, I am!" He's got a little family and is completely crazy about his kids. He'll show you a hundred pictures of them if you let him corner you. He's all about his wife and family. He's also deeply committed to his church and his faith. Those are the things that matter to him, and his work is the path to making sure they're well cared for and supported.

All the guys of this group are on the same page regarding their priorities, and they're all rock stars in the company, every one of them. I'm not a deeply spiritual person, but I have a tremendous amount of respect for people who have spirituality and use it in a positive way. And these guys use their belief system to give them peace and direction. It might not work for everyone, but it sure works for them.

Why are they so successful? Because they've got goals that are deeply rooted in who they are and what they believe, not some goals they arbitrarily set or borrowed from someone else, but goals with meaning that reflect who they are.

Their families are the center of their lives. They're all committed to nurturing their spiritual lives and to being active, contributing members of their faith community. And they all want to make money at a high level to support those very important components of their lives. Their work has meaning because their lives have meaning—and the work supports that. Those things are their drivers, so meeting their goals is an act of love and faith, not a slog. And they wake up every day, happy to go to work and ready to win. That mindset propels their success.

What propels you? What really matters to you? Who told you so? Is your goal organic, springing out of who you are and what you value, or was it handed to you, drummed into you, or something you just fell back on by default?

If you don't know the answer to that, you're going to need to do the work it takes to figure it out.

Work on It

People who consistently fail at meeting their goals are all really good at making one thing: excuses. They fall off their diets because they went on a cruise, and they couldn't push away from the buffet. They fall off the wagon because a friend got married, and they had to toast the happy couple. They miss the mark at work—making the calls they need to make or whatever it was—because the dog ate their to-do list, and they just didn't get around to it. They're short on successes but long on reasons why it's not their fault.

Does this sound uncomfortably familiar to you?

- Take a minute—nobody's going to judge you. I want you to think a little bit, then write down three excuses you make to yourself or to others about why you failed to make your goal. Doesn't matter what the goal is.
- I'll wait.
- Now take a critical look at each of them. What was it that you didn't follow through on? What did that cost you?
- In what areas of your life do you find yourself making excuses regularly? Work? Home? Self-care?
- What does that tell you about your feelings toward the areas in which you're not consistently meeting your own goals?
- And what's the real, underlying reason you didn't do what you had said you wanted to do, what you meant to do, or what you promised to do?

Yes, everyone fails sometimes. Sometimes you're sick, or someone's in trouble, or the car breaks down, or whatever. But if you're consistently making excuses when you should be meeting goals, you need to figure out why. Something's out of balance—and I'd bet it's to be found in the tension between your stated goals and your genuine commitment to them.

To the Point

- If you're consistently failing to measure up to the goals you've set, something interior is undermining you. In my experience that's usually because your goals aren't really what you want, so you're not stimulated to make the efforts you need to make to succeed.

- If you're not committed to your goals, why not? Chances are they don't connect to who you really are and what you actually want.

- Examine your goals in life. List them out. Are they really yours, or are they ones you inherited from your parents? Absorbed from your peers? Were taught you should hold?

- Do your goals conflict with each other? Remember Lucy? Her goals were both good ones, but her life situation meant that she had to choose one and wait for the other. She wisely chose what mattered most to her and is now enjoying her success at meeting her professional goals. Why? Because she wasn't being pulled in two competing directions.

- If you realize that you're in the habit of making excuses for failing to meet your goals, you need to consider why.

- Self-awareness is critical to good goal setting and follow-through. You can't commit to something that doesn't resonate with who you are and what you really want.

CHAPTER TWO

Put Yourself First

Susan had a rough childhood by anybody's standards. Her parents had issues—anger, substance abuse—and were too busy slugging it out between themselves to give her the kind of attention and support a kid needs while growing up. Her mostly absent father treated her mother like crap when he came around, so that was her understanding of what marriage looked like. It was almost as if her and her mother's roles were reversed; it was Susan who comforted her mom after a bout with Dad. When her mom was overwhelmed, she'd dump Susan and her brother with whatever family member would take them. She looked for attention in all the wrong places, falling in with a bad crew.

She fell in love with a thug who treated her the same way her father had treated her mom. She allowed it, because she had no sense of her own value, and the idea of putting her needs ahead of someone else's was not in her frame of reference. Before long she had two kids of her own, an incarcerated partner, and problems keeping her kids in line. Not surprisingly the ongoing drama of her family life—who's in trouble, who's in jail, who's going to show up drunk and break the place up—were all absorbing. Eventually her kids left home, and it was just her.

That's when she showed up to apply for an entry-level job with us. She didn't have a lot of skills, but now, with her family issues off of her shoulders and more time to concentrate on herself, she'd discovered a spark of drive and ambition and a strong desire to do better, to create a career and security that didn't depend on someone else. As someone who'd had his own issues growing up in a dysfunctional family, I understood where she was coming from. We'd talk from time to time, and something I tried to impress on her was that she needed to finally put herself first. Everyone else's needs or problems had come ahead of hers up until now. She was on the cusp of creating a new and better life for herself, one in which she could be a success and enjoy peace and security for the first time. Could she break the habits she had of letting others push her around physically and emotionally and work on making a better life for Susan?

She could and did. You could literally see the changes in her as she gradually came out of her shell and took her place in the sun. Her appearance changed—she lost weight, made time for herself to exercise, got her hair styled. Her body language changed—she stood straighter, looked people in the eye, and smiled more. Her me-first attitude was paying dividends, and her life view grew more optimistic and positive. She'd started at rock bottom. Now, she's the leader of a successful sales group. She's mentoring other women who are coming into the business with issues similar to hers, helping them get past those emotional stumbling blocks and on their feet. She's a rock star.

What was the change that made it all possible? She'd learned to put herself first. She realized that there was more to life for her than coping with the fallout from other people's problems and trying to fix them. She was done with that—and ready to take care of herself.

Was it selfish of her to concentrate on getting healthy, learning the business, polishing her professional presentation? Nope, but initially that was her reaction to the idea. I don't like to generalize, but in my observation, this is harder for women to do than it is for men. Why? I think women are encouraged to be self-sacrificing; the image of the sainted mother giving her all for her kids is familiar from books and movies. And there's nothing wrong with giving—but if you don't fill your own cup first, you're not going to have anything to give.

That's why this is what I tell my coaching clients and the groups I speak to: Number one, you take care of yourself. Number two, you take care of your spouse. Number three, you take care of your kids. Number four, you take care of your soul, and work is number five.

Why Must You Put Yourself First?

If you want to be a success—in business or in private life—you have to start prioritizing your own well-being, even if that goes against the grain of what you've been taught and the examples you've seen in your family. People praise those who put others ahead of themselves: "Oh, Susan's such a do-gooder. She's never thinking about herself. She's always doing things for other people. She's so amazing," putting that person up on a pedestal. And yeah, that's great for as long as it lasts—great for other people, not for Susan, because she's eventually going to crumble under the pressure. You just can't live life that way.

I'm all for giving back and helping; I've built a foundation to enable me to do exactly that. But only after you've taken care of yourself and your family, then there's plenty of time to give back to the community. First, you have to get yourself squared away. If you're not happy, you can't take care of your significant other. You can't do a great job with your kids. You can't do a great job at work or as a member of your community. You can't live in your faith if you're unhappy and screwed up.

That's why you have to start with *number one*—you. Nobody else can or will do it for you.

How Are Things at Home?

The way you live—what you go home to every night—has a lot to do with how happy you are. Take a hard look at your home life and see if it's supporting you or holding you down. If you're unhappy at home, you're not going to succeed in your job. You may have learned to swallow the dysfunctional behavior in your home life; it can even give you an adrenaline charge because you take your focus off your personal life and only focus on your business life, but that falls apart because of the internal pressure it creates.

Maybe you prioritize others' well-being ahead of your own at home. I've worked with many who struggle with this, mostly my female colleagues who think their kids are more important than they are. You can't do that if you hope to succeed! You can't put your kids ahead of yourself for several good reasons. First, that's not your job. Your job as a parent is to give them love, support, and a good example of how to be an adult. That's it. If you're modeling putting kids first, you're not providing a great example for them to follow in adulthood. Second, they're not going to be with you forever, so they can't be everything you're about. They're only part of what you're about. Third, if you're providing for them, you've got to put yourself at the top of the food chain, because when your needs are met and you have happiness and some serenity, you'll be a better parent and the kids will turn out better.

My good friend Diane is one of those highly capable people who believed that her primary duty was to her kids. Her marriage to an abusive spouse had broken up, and he was out of the picture. Her three sons were the focus of her energy and efforts, and almost miraculously she was able to raise them all through their teen years without them going through the angry, acting-out phase so many fatherless boys experience. She was able to do it thanks to her tremendous emotional intelligence, her ability to listen to them, really hear their concerns, and give good advice. She modeled caring, calm, and a great work ethic—and her boys absorbed it. They behaved themselves even under peer pressure because they respected and loved Mom and didn't want to disappoint her.

But there was a cost to her in terms of her career. She was a smart, savvy businesswoman, but she wasn't focusing her attention on herself, and that held her back from getting jobs that were really worth her time. Once her boys were old enough, she began her career in earnest, starting up a small business on her own that grew to real success. It was demanding and ate up her attention and labor 24/7, but the reward was a thriving enterprise that provided well for her and her employees and a deeply loyal base of repeat customers.

Why did she do so well? Because she'd finally seen that she needed to put herself first. Once she did that, success was almost inevitable. The lesson here is that if you're committed to putting yourself first—to putting your own wellness and happiness first—you're going to be a better partner and set a powerful example for your kids.

If your home life is toxic or chaotic, if you're stuck in a miserable relationship with someone for whom you no longer care, or with someone who's abusive, or one in which chemical dependence is an issue—how in the world are you going to be able to give your career the attention it needs to flourish? You're not. You'll be too busy caring for others, putting out fires, or trying to make everyone happy. They won't be, and you won't be.

How's Your Health?

Once you start looking at your life through the lens of putting yourself first, you've got to commit to taking care of yourself. What that looks like depends on what you're doing—or not doing—now.

For me, my substance abuse came to define every part of my life. My expectation of life was that I'd wake up, start drinking, and keep drinking until I passed out. I had a lot of free-floating rage that even the booze couldn't numb, so part of my life was looking for outlets for those feelings.

This was my usual Saturday night. Typically, I'd walk into a bar and look for two things: first, a woman I wanted to hit on and take home; and second, a guy I could beat up if the woman wasn't interested. I wish I was kidding, but I'm not. If I struck out with the girl, I'd find a way to pick a fight with the guy—I'd knock into him or start making cracks about his clothes or looks or whatever—then purge that boiling anger out of my system by beating the crap out of him.

My problems were double edged—alcoholism and clinical depression that I expressed through those violent outbursts. I dealt with the alcoholism by joining AA, getting with the program, and staying sober. The depression was a tougher one for me, because I didn't want to admit I had a mental health issue. I didn't see any problem. I liked fighting; it gave me a charge. I'd grown up fighting recreationally with my gang, looking for chances to get into it with whoever got in my way or just rubbed me the wrong way. It was great—until it wasn't.

Unfortunately for me and for a lot of guys I came into contact with over the years, it wasn't until I was middle aged that I realized I was risking everything I valued—my relationship with my wife and family, my business, my reputation—by being the kind of guy who'd take road rage to the extreme, force someone to pull over if they cut me off, and just bang their head in their car door until I got my point across. With the blessing of my therapist, I went on antidepressants, and thanks to that and therapy, this kind of garbage is mostly in the rearview, and I'm a happy man.

If you know or even suspect you've got a substance abuse problem, get help, and get sober. I can guarantee you that if you don't, you'll never really achieve what should be your ultimate objective: real happiness, real serenity, and success as you define it. Had I stayed a drunk, I'd not have any of the things that matter to me, certainly not the happy marriage and family life that make my life so rich nor the business I enjoy too much to give up. I'd probably be in a tent on Venice Beach or, more likely, dead. Without getting sober there was zero chance of me changing my behavior. If you don't get sober, you won't ever know what it is to be your best self. You won't be able to experience the rewards that come by doing.

Mental health is a complex subject and one that too many of us shy away from discussing when it comes to ourselves, but I can't stress enough how important it is to your happiness and your success that you deal with it decisively, that you seek help for whatever chemical dependency, depression, fears, anger—any of the negative things that can and will derail you if they go unchecked—you may be laboring under. There's help available, and the only shame is in not seeking it out if you need it. I cannot tell you how important finding the right therapist has been for me. But I can guarantee that I wouldn't be the happy man I am if I hadn't done it.

Another part of putting yourself first is taking care of your body. I'm not talking about getting buffed up like an action hero but just making time for exercise and committing to getting it done, on a set schedule every week. Exercise does more than make you feel stronger, lower your blood pressure, and keep the twinges in the hinges at bay— though it certainly does all that. It's a great release from tension and floods your brain with the feel-good brain chemicals, dopamine and serotonin, that help to relieve stress and anxiety and lift your mood. Even if it did only that, the effort would be worth it. But you'll look better, feel younger, and have more energy, which will further support your attitude upgrade and make liking yourself that much easier.

How's Your Attitude?

Speaking of attitude, I believe that how we choose to look at our daily life is a huge predictor of happiness and success, and I also believe that we can purposefully adjust our attitude in ways that will make those good things more immediately accessible. People tend to think that their attitude is a product of what's happening to them at a given moment. But my belief is that the opposite is true. What we put out there—with our attitude, our self-talk, the ways in which we frame our daily experiences—is what we get back, in terms of how we interact with the world. It's a choice, whether you know it or not.

I can get up in the morning and think, "Ah, hell, I've got to get up and go to the damn office." When I get there, I can bring that negative attitude with me and inflict it on the people who work with me. Alternatively, I can get up and make a point of saying, "I get to go to work today and interact with all these people I like. Lucky me!"

On the days my exercise coach comes, I can grumble about having to get up and roll around on the floor and do all the stuff she inflicts on me, or I can be happy about it and grateful that I've got a great coach to help me accomplish what I want to, and I choose happy. I tend to fall into habits I find comfortable. There's a particular restaurant I like to go to for lunch. Nothing fancy, just a good, simple spot where I can sit with a newspaper and read while I eat. For some people that would be boring, but for me it's bliss. I get to eat something I like (and have ordered hundreds of times) and enjoy the paper. And I think about that and how lucky I am for this small but satisfying pleasure. When I drive to work on a sunny day, I put the top down on the car and just dig the day. It's a choice—to take the small things as blessings that add up to a great life. It's all in how you look at it.

If your self-talk isn't up to par—if you're habitually negative and looking for the half-empty glass—fix it. "Habitually" is the key word here because it *is* a habit, and habits can be changed. Get in the gratitude habit, and when you catch yourself talking things down, stop and flip

WHAT WE PUT OUT THERE—WITH OUR ATTITUDE, OUR SELF-TALK, THE WAYS IN WHICH WE FRAME OUR DAILY EXPERI-ENCES—IS WHAT WE GET BACK, IN TERMS OF HOW WE INTERACT WITH THE WORLD. IT'S A CHOICE, WHETHER YOU KNOW IT OR NOT.

the script. Look for the good stuff and say it out loud. Celebrate what you're doing, what you have, even if it's just a sunny day and an egg sandwich. Before you know it, your self-talk will change your world view. Sounds goofy, but it works.

Take Responsibility for Your Happiness

Or your unhappiness.

There are always going to be people to blame for how you are, how you view the world or your place in it—your parents, that girlfriend or boyfriend who dumped you, your peers, society's ills, whatever—who contributed to your sorry state.

But here's the deal. Until you let go of that—forgive those who wronged you and take responsibility for yourself going forward— you're screwed, and you'll stay screwed. You're mired in anger and resentment. And all those people who did you wrong? They're living rent-free in your head.

At one point in my life, I wound up locked up in what I can only describe as a mental institution for thirty-five days of drying out and treatment. It wasn't my first choice—I mean, I'd sooner have been in Cancun—but it beat jail time, and by the time I left I was able to accept that I was the one who was responsible for my winding up there. I couldn't do it without help. That bugged me, but I swallowed it because it was clearly the truth. Being incarcerated and doing a lot of drugs and alcohol wasn't working out as a life plan; I knew it would eventually either kill me or get me locked up for longer.

Being in treatment is not fun. But if you make up your mind that you're going to take something from it and watch what's going on around you, you might come out better than you went in. And so, after a period of time, I accepted the fact that I wanted to be sober. I figured if it didn't work out and I wasn't happier, then piss on sobriety; I'd hitchhike out to California and live on Skid Row.

Never made it to California—at least, not as a bum.

I was lucky; not everybody gets a positive reaction with sobriety. Some people continue to battle, some lose their job, and their relationships go to hell. Sobriety will eventually feel normal to them, but in the short term it feels alien and lousy, and they often fall back into booze and drugs. For me, though, it felt right. I was ready for it. I got a real job, and I bought my first house and fixed it up. And after I fixed it up, I thought, "Hmm, maybe you should get a real estate license and list it yourself." And that's how I got into real estate. That house led to another house, and another—and so it went.

Why did it work? Because I decided to put on my big boy pants and take responsibility for my life, my choices, and my happiness.

And I did it by putting myself first.

Did You Get Screwed? Get Used to It.

It's happened to me countless times, and it will happen to you. Maybe you've been building a relationship with a prospect and you're feeling really great about it. They're about to list, and you just know that listing's going to you. You've done everything right, you're on the same page, and they're going to sign with you. You're practically banking your commission.

Then you go on your computer and discover they've listed with someone else.

What happened? How could they have led you along?

Maybe someone was better at closing than you are. Maybe they didn't like you as much as you thought. Maybe that other person just happened to be there at the right time. You'll probably never know. Like I said, it's part of the business. I courted a prospect with sports tickets for months, expecting he'd list with me. I'd known him most of my life, and I'd sold several houses for him, so it seemed like a reasonable expectation. But you know who I didn't talk to? His wife.

I called him one day to ask if he wanted some tickets for an upcoming game—and, unexpectedly, he told me I needed to talk to his wife and handed the phone to her. She told me, "We signed a contract with another agent."

If you're in sales, you get screwed all the time. If you're in relationships, you get screwed all the time. If you have kids, you get screwed all the time. It just happens. Your kids are not necessarily going to meet your standards for them all the time. They're going to go in a direction you wish they wouldn't, ignoring your advice. You will have periods where you wonder, "What's wrong with them? What's wrong with me? What did I do wrong?" That's going to happen, and it's going to lead to periods of self-reflection where you examine whatever negative thing has occurred and consider what you should have done to avoid it. But you can't spend your life looking in the rearview. You've got to accept that sometimes we just don't get what we want and move ahead, because, in fact, not everything is within our ability to control.

That's what's so brilliant about the Serenity Prayer; it acknowledges that there are things we can't control and leads us to let those things go. That's putting yourself first, because getting mired in what's gone wrong will slow you down. Take whatever lessons you've learned—I should have put more effort into making friends with my friend's wife, for instance—and keep moving forward.

The same thing goes for your employees. You've got to look at the big picture of their performance, not the small, day-to-day errors everyone is going to make. They have lives outside of work, distractions and issues and worries that will inevitably absorb their attention. If they're winning 80 percent of the time, though, they're rock stars. And you let that 20 percent where they're not winning go, and you encourage them to let it go too. Why? Because hindsight is great, and you can learn from it—but none of it matters if you don't move forward and move on. If you dwell on it, let it embitter you, or let your failures define you going forward, you're holding yourself back.

Here's the thing: you've got to prioritize. Like I said at the top of this chapter, your happiness is number one. The second most important is your spouse's or significant other's happiness. The third is your kids. Fourth comes your spiritual life, whatever that looks like. Work and career are fifth.

Why that order? If you're not happy, none of these other people or things are going to prosper. If your spouse isn't happy, it's going to interfere with your happiness and with the happiness of your children. If your kids aren't happy, that's going to make you miserable too. If you're not spiritually centered in some meaningful way—if you're not in touch with something that gives you a sense of peace and your place in the world—you've got fewer resources to fall back on when the hard times hit. And your career and work won't prosper unless you've got all those other things sorted out first.

That's why you put yourself first. Doesn't sound so selfish now, right?

Work on It

Now that you (hopefully) understand why it's so important to put yourself first, let's take a look at some of the ways you might be failing to do that and what you can do differently:

- Are you a doormat? People who are doormats put everyone ahead of themselves. Maybe it's what you were told you were supposed to do while growing up. Maybe you're just too shy to speak up. But if you find yourself having what should be others' responsibilities thrust on you or carrying the weight for someone who can't be bothered to pick it up himself, it's time to get up off the floor and change that.

- Start with saying no. The power of "no" can't be underestimated, and there's nothing negative about it. Someone wants you to do something that's not your responsibility, something they're supposed to do themselves. Maybe it's a one-time thing, so you're willing to help out—but what happens when the one time turns into every time? Say "no." No more, *no más*. Something like, "I've been happy to help you out with this, but I don't have the time to do your work as well as my own. You're going to have to find another way to get it done." When you're asked to give or do more than you can handle, and it's clearly above and beyond what should be your responsibilities, say "no." Believe me, the more you do this, the lighter you'll feel, and the easier saying "no" gets. Practice makes perfect.

- If your relationship is causing you heartache, act. Don't hope it will get better, take action to make it better or end it. Couples therapy is a great place to start. If your partner refuses to go, go on your own and get the insights and support you need to do what you need to do, even if that means ending the relationship. Don't go through life with a partner who makes you miserable. Again, getting the weight of that off your shoulders is going to make you feel ten times lighter.

- If you're not taking responsibility for your health, now is the time and today is the day you start. Make a list. Be brutal. What health issues that are under your control need to be addressed? What exactly will it take to fix them? If that means facing chemical dependency and seeking help, do it. If it means losing weight or getting into shape, get help with that.

There are plenty of doctors, coaches, and organizations that can steer you in the right direction and provide the accountability you need to stay on track. Whatever is keeping you from doing this—sloth, lack of self-esteem, or self-doubt—shove that aside and write down concrete steps you can take, along with a timeline for taking them.

To the Point

- Lists are a great way to prioritize your own needs. I make a list every week of the calls I have to make, the meetings I have to take, and what I need to get done. That list gets addressed without fail. That means on the weekends I can take the time I need to relax and unwind without stressing over what I didn't get done—because it all got done. It sounds tough, but it beats beating myself up or worrying over what I missed. A list is a great tool. Use it.

- Look at what and who you prioritize now. If you're not at the top of your list, why not? How can you change that? Sometimes it's just habit. Habits can be changed, as long as we're conscious of them. I talked above about how doing someone a favor can turn into your job if you let it become a regular thing. If you're not carving out "me time" for yourself, now is a good time to start.

- What makes you happy? What relaxes you, relieves stress? For me it's coming home to my cat and hanging out together on the couch. For you it might be taking a run or going fishing or having a catch with your kid. Whatever it is, make time for it and schedule that time deliberately so you're not tempted to put it off.

- Look at the big picture of what you want—and make a plan that will support you in getting there, on a workable, realistic schedule. What must you do to move ahead? Break it down, write it down, get it done. Day-to-day thinking leaves you struggling to keep up with the little stuff, but you have to have a sense of where you're going so you're not spinning your wheels. Consider meeting with a coach or a mentor who's where you want to be and getting their advice. Make an investment in your success.

CHAPTER THREE

Wanting to Want

Gerry was a larger-than-life kind of a guy, with a big personality, big smile, and big ambitions. When we first sat down together, he shared that he basically wanted to be me when he grew up, a leader in sales and in the company. Clearly, he had the people skills to make it happen and a sincere interest in others that most people found captivating. He had a quick, restless intelligence and loved to read—a trait I appreciate in people, since I'm a big reader myself. On paper he had everything going for him to make a bundle in real estate, which is at bottom a people business, not a house business.

What wasn't so immediately apparent was that his follow-through didn't match his ambition. He was great at making plans but lousy at implementing them in any consistent way. He'd do everything I suggested—make lists, make phone calls, follow up, keep in contact with his prospects—but only for a while. Then he'd drop the ball. Somehow something else inevitably came up that distracted his attention from where it needed to be.

It befuddles me why the steps to be successful are clear and generally understood. That means that when people choose not to follow them, they're actually choosing to fail as opposed to choosing to succeed. It's a conscious decision. You don't sell houses by hanging around your house in your underwear. It doesn't work like that, or everyone would do it.

Our conversation went like this: "John, I want to sell more houses. What do I need to do?"

"Start with a plan and work it. Work it every week, without fail."

So we laid out a plan. He'd make so many cold calls a week, so many follow-up calls a week, and so on. And he always started out with tremendous enthusiasm, coming to the coaching classes regularly to report on his activity level. Turns out he was fibbing, because he didn't want to look like a dunce in front of other people. Not only was he not putting in the time, but he was lying about it, which had to have caused him a lot of internal conflict.

When I called him on it, he was understandably embarrassed. He dropped out of the class pretty quickly after that. Why? It was easier to avoid what he saw as my judgment of him than to face his weaknesses and work the plan. That's the difference between simply wanting something and *wanting* to want it.

Why Do We Plan?

We plan because it's how stuff gets done. I get up and meet my exercise coach three times a week because it's on my calendar. I could call her and tell her I wasn't feeling well, turn off the alarm, and go back to sleep. I'd much rather do that. But that's not how great careers or great relationships or even passable muscle tone is accomplished. So I get up, get dressed, and meet with her—because that's my plan.

When I sit down with a client to craft a business plan, I start with some very straightforward questions:

- Number one, what's your plan for taking care of yourself? What do you need to do to work on you?
- What do you need to do to support your relationship with your significant other?
- What do you need to do to be there for your family?
- What do you need to do to fulfill your spiritual needs?

Once you take care of all of those, you're going to thrive at work. In my view people usually fail to meet their ambitions because they don't address these questions in a substantive way or in the proper order.

But those are the big things. Simple stuff can also screw you up—not getting up at a regular time in the morning, for instance, even though you know that it's just better for you if you have a fixed schedule of when you go to bed and get up. That's common sense; it's good for your body, it's good for your brain, and it enhances your productivity. The quality and quantity of sleep you get, what you eat, how much you exercise—these are all things that impact your well-being and help you stay on top of your game. The same goes for the work schedule you create for yourself. In the case of real estate, making calls is critical to success, and again, it's got to be on a schedule you set and stick to. Why? Because if you let it slide once, it gets easier to let it slide the second time.

All this boils down to making a lifestyle plan that works for you and using that to help you build your business plan. The demographic I typically see struggling with this are those who are somewhere in their first five years of working in this goofy business. I'm not saying that someone who's been in it for fifteen years doesn't sometimes slip and need to regroup or retrain, only that it more often happens to those in the first phase of their careers.

My own first year in the business is a good example of what I'm talking about. When I got my first job in an "old school" real estate office, I'd already gotten some clients lined up, so I went from brand new to being the third-best agent in about three months. I was killing it. But I wasn't building my business because I wasn't doing any prospecting. When the business I had lined up as a rookie dried up, I was done. I lacked the willingness to prospect when I first started in the business, because I thought I

YOU HAVE TO HOLD SOME KIND OF VISION OF WHERE YOUR EFFORTS ARE GOING AND EMBRACE WHAT IT TAKES TO GET THERE.

had it made. My attitude was, "The buyers came out of the woodwork before. I'm bound to get more." Unfortunately, they didn't keep coming out of the woodwork. I had to learn how to knock on a door and pick up a phone, and it took a while to get that into my system.

That's why I drum it into my agents and my coaching clients who want to know why they're not making money: How many contacts did you make today? How many prospects did you identify? How many appointments did you go out on? And if you tell me the truth about your efforts over three to four weeks, I'll be able to predict with fair accuracy how many houses you're going to sell. It's just that simple.

Why Simply "Wanting" Isn't Enough

It's not enough to have a desire to accomplish great things. You have to have a desire to want to get better at what you do, in order to accomplish those things. You've got to want to do the work it takes to achieve what you want.

You have to hold some kind of vision of where your efforts are going and embrace what it takes to get there.

After I'd been going to AA meetings for a while, I got to where I could pick the ones who'd more likely succeed at getting sober from among the many who came to a few meetings then sort of faded away. The ones who made it were motivated to want to make it—by things that really mattered to them but ultimately by being honest with themselves about where the path they were on inevitably led if they didn't sober up. Yes, their marriage was on the rocks, and maybe if they committed to sobriety the wife might let them back into the house. Yep, their job was on the line too, and the boss had to see they meant it about getting straight. Maybe they wanted their driver's license back.

This is why so many people go to treatment and fail. The percentage is huge of how many people will use drugs or alcohol within three years. And it isn't that the treatment sucks—it's that they never really wanted to quit, didn't have that depth of desire to quit. They didn't want to be in jail anymore, and they'd kind of like to get their driver's license back, and maybe they'd just as soon not get divorced, so they'd like to quit for those reasons. But the hardcore reason—the priority of "Number one, I want to be sober"—isn't what's driving their desire. Almost always, they use again. I can't tell you how many times I've seen that in AA.

How to Want to Want

There's a method to getting there, starting with this:

YOU MUST HAVE A WILLINGNESS TO LEARN

Without it, you'll never be able to move forward.

I missed out on a lot of information that was presented to me throughout my life, because I wasn't in a situation in which I wanted to learn or to change my behavior. When I was an addict, I knew I was an addict. Given the course I was on, my assumption was that, ultimately, I was going to be a bum. That was the realistic outcome I had to look forward to, because that's what my actions were leading me to.

When I started to get sober and my mind began to function the way it should, I went back to a habit I'd dropped a long time previously, the habit of reading. I'm a nonfiction fan, and I'm interested in what successful people have to say about how they got that way. I'm interested in stories of failure too, failure on a small, personal scale or on a big, governmental or historical scale. Everything I read opens up and improves my understanding of the world and makes me better at what I do.

I was willing to learn how to sell real estate and to take on the work that learning entailed—to relish it, honestly, because I knew it would buy me the independence I wanted. Getting good at it was an ongoing process for years, and even now I go to speaking events to hear people talk about how they made it in the business. Maybe I know 98 percent of what they had to say already, but there was always something new to hear, a novel way of looking at an issue that helps me get clarity.

There are many necessary activities to selling more houses, many of which suck—the prospecting, the difficult clients, the tough closings. There are a lot of things that are no fun that are part of the job description. But when you see that paycheck after a big sale, you're feeling pretty good, especially lately with average sale prices just soaring, because you make a lot of money. Even though money is worth less than it used to be, on average, a real estate agent makes more money now than they did five years ago because of the average sale price escalating.

That said, you have to have the desire to stick with it and the willingness to learn and change. If you're doing the same things for your clients that you were doing ten years ago, you're dead. You've got to change your marketing materials and look at new ways to reach out. One of my newer hires is always changing it up, and it's really working for him and for us. He decided to throw an ice cream social in one of our office parking lots and invited all his clients to come and bring the kids. His wife and baby were there, and he was a great host, making everyone feel at home and talking to them about their needs and plans. It cost a little money and a fair amount of effort, but it was more than worth the good will and better relationships he got from it. This business is built on relationships, and we can all learn more about how to cultivate them in a way that feels natural and good to us.

I take my relationships with my employees seriously too and do everything I can to make them feel appreciated. The handwritten notes, the quick, friendly check-ins at their desks—I want them to know that I'm a happy and optimistic person, not some grumpy jerk, because if I'm affirming that, I'm affirming their choice to be there working with me. That was learned behavior for me, and I've been doing it so long and so consciously that it's become my nature. I've grown into the role I have now because I never stopped learning and taking in other ways to see the world and be present in it.

DON'T STOP LEARNING. IF YOU'RE OUT OF THE HABIT, START NOW.

Don't stop learning. If you're out of the habit, start now. Seek out coaches and mentors, authors, and speakers who can inform you and help you reshape your relationship to how to get to where you want to be.

YOU MUST NOT ACCEPT MEDIOCRITY

Begin to embrace your full potential.

This seems so obvious to me now, although it wasn't always the case. Mediocrity would have been a big step up for me from where I was at my lowest point. But I lost my taste for it when I realized I didn't have to settle for pretty good; I could soar.

I don't know why people accept mediocrity or unhappiness in the areas that matter to them. I mean, think of the people we all know who are living in miserable marriages they'd love to be out of. I don't know about you, but I think it's nuts to live with somebody for twenty years, nineteen of those after you've figured out you'd be happier alone. Fix the marriage or get divorced! There's no obligation to be there. You come first, your relationship comes second, and your kids come third, so if you stay in a relationship that sucks, and you're miserable, you ain't doing anybody any favors.

The same goes for the other aspects of your life, from self-care to work. If you don't care enough to reject "so-so" and go after "great," why are you even reading this book?

Last year our real estate company was given an award as the biggest and best RE/MAX agency in the world. We outsold every other group. But this year there's another RE/MAX that bought up a whole bunch of offices, and they sold about two thousand more houses than we did. That shouldn't bug me—but it does. The impulse to push ahead that helped me build the company still gave me a little nudge when I heard this. A little voice said, "Okay, we're not done growing. We'll do some acquisitions." That voice won't shut up, even though I've largely stepped back from the day-to-day operations and put someone else in charge, and she's doing a great job.

Does it bug me a little when I go to the office and see a meeting of the company officers happening that I wasn't invited to? Yes, reflexively—because it's hard to shed the habit of commitment and the sense of ownership. Those feelings didn't allow for shoulder shrugs on my part, or for mediocrity, which is why I can afford to pull back and apply my drive to the things that matter to me now.

ADMIT YOUR FAULTS AND BE WILLING TO COMMIT TO DOING BETTER

If you can't do this, you're just going to keep on pulling yourself down and pulling down those around you as you go along.

Here's an example. I used to attend meetings at an AA group that was created to accommodate those of us who don't believe in God or deities generally but can embrace the idea of an abstract higher power. It was a great group, and I got a lot out of the meetings. But it fell apart, because guys trying to get out of going to jail for substance abuse–connected crimes would tell the judges that they couldn't go to AA because they were atheists, so the judges would sentence them to come to our meeting. Why did this lead to the demise of what had been a good group? Because these guys weren't committed. They didn't want to quit; they didn't want to get better. They didn't want to take on the next challenge in front of them of figuring out sobriety and turning it into a good thing. They just wanted to get their attendance card signed so they could stay out of jail.

The most important things in life take real commitment. Getting sober is one of them, because it requires you to get honest with yourself and with those around you. It requires you to take action and to be accountable for your behavior going forward. It requires you to admit where you've failed, without equivocating, and to commit to doing better.

Oh, and by the way, there's no way someone else can genuinely motivate you to commit to something. That has to come from inside of you. If you think you can pay your money and go hear a motivational speaker tell you something that's going to make you able to throw yourself, heart and soul, to some new, better direction, you're wasting your money. Nobody can turn your life around except you.

BE SURE YOU KNOW WHAT YOU REALLY WANT

This sounds like a no-brainer, but seriously I meet a lot of people who talk a big game but fail to follow through with the work it takes to win, because they're not clear on what they want. They know what they think they want, or what someone has told them they should want, but they don't get there, because it's not in their hearts.

What do you want? Where are you going? Do you want to be single, playing the field? Do you want to be a financier? Do you want to be a person hitchhiking around America? Do you want to go to Europe and hitchhike around? What's your dream? That's the first part, knowing the truth of that, because then you'll put real energy into figuring out how to get there. Say I want to bum around Europe for a long stretch, backpacking and seeing the sights. That's going to motivate me to work hard for five years and spend no extra money. I'm going to live really frugally. I'm going to save $32,000. Then I'm going to go to Europe and hitchhike until the money's gone. I know if I do those things—if I commit to the plan and work it—my dream will come true, and I'm willing to work hard and sacrifice over a long term to make it happen.

Something may come along that challenges that plan and my commitment to it. I might be offered a big promotion at work, but accepting the new job means that I no longer have the option to take off. Or my wife might say she doesn't want me to go and make it a condition of staying in the marriage. If those things happen, I've got to weigh what matters more to me—to figure out what I really want—and prioritize that, because I'm my own number one priority. If I'm miserable because I traded my dream for a bigger paycheck or a relationship I don't care as much about, I'm no good to me, my job, or my wife.

Work on It

The process of wanting to want is not a one-and-done but an ongoing effort at serious self-assessment that keeps you continually moving forward. Your goals will change as you achieve them and go after new ones, but wanting to want an achievement will always be the only way you can reliably make it. Start now, and don't stop. There's always another worthy goal on the horizon.

My wants have changed as my life has progressed. I've got all the money I'll ever need, and then some. I've got a great wife, a cat, and a car collection. I do look at cars all the time online, so it's not impossible that I will be an idiot and buy another car.

But what I want is to have the feeling that I had this morning when I got up and worked out, then hopped in my car and thought,

"It's a nice day today. I'm going to have a good one. It's a nice day today. I just feel good."

That's all I want, and that's a choice I've made and make every day. People don't take the responsibility for making those kinds of choices. But if you're bored or unhappy, those are choices too. Yes, each of us will face challenges to our choice to be happy.

There are also challenges you can't do a thing about. As I write this, my best friend is dying. I've been visiting him regularly, and when he's gone, I'll do what I can to help his family. But right now, the reality for him is misery, misery he didn't choose, and it tears me up to see him suffer. But I can't do anything about it, and I've accepted that. I've done a lot of things for him, as his health has deteriorated. I'm there for him. We have been best friends for fifty years. There's nothing left we can do except for me to be there for him when he wants me. But when he dies, I'm not going to waste time grieving or put flowers on his grave. It won't help him, and it will hurt me. I'm doing my grieving now, but once his suffering is over, I'm going to let go, because I don't want to carry negativity or sorrow around. That's not good for me, and it won't help him. Instead, I'm taking the energy I'd use in sorrow over my loss and channeling it into helping others through my foundation. That's worth wanting and a meaningful legacy for me to leave behind when I go.

To the Point

How can we best structure our efforts toward wanting to want?

- *Be honest with yourself.* If you don't really lust after the goal you've set, you've set the wrong goal. You've got to want to reach it wholeheartedly. That's the only kind of goal worth chasing. Make sure that your goals are genuinely yours, not someone else's idea of what you should want. Then go for it.

- *Have a plan.* Planning is critical to success, because without having a logical series of actions in mind that will move you forward, you're just flailing around and wasting your time and energy. Remember the guy who wanted to get to Europe and backpack across it? He had a plan—he established that it would cost him X number of dollars to go, X number of years to work and save, and X number of dollars he'd put away from his earnings that would allow him to go. Make a plan as solid and straightforward as that and commit to it.

- *Share your plan.* Who do you share your plan with? It could be your significant other, or it could be your coach, your boss, or all of them. Sharing it helps you to be clear about the details and sound out the specifics with someone whose judgment you respect. They might have some ideas that could help, and they might not, but saying your plan out loud will help you to see it more clearly and enhance your commitment to it.

- *Establish accountability.* Part of the reason you share your plan with someone is that it helps to create accountability. In an ideal world, we'd all be so motivated to get what we're after that we wouldn't need anyone's support, oversight, or nudging. But nobody's perfect, so we have accountability partners to help us hold ourselves to the mark we've set.

CHAPTER FOUR

Doing the Necessary Introspection

My then-fiancée now-wife was with me in the car one afternoon when a couple of guys were tailgating me then cut me off. To be blunt, I lost it. I caught up with them, forced their car to the side of the road, pulled the driver out of the car, and banged his head into the door until he stopped fighting back. The guy in the passenger's seat should have made a better choice than to get out and come at me, but people make a lot of errors in judgment, so this was not his best day either.

Me? I felt great. My fiancée? Not so much. She made that clear when I got back into the car.

"If you ever do that again when I'm with you, we're done." I agreed to that condition—plenty of wiggle room built into it, after all, since it didn't cover when she *wasn't* with me—but it wasn't until a while later (and several more of those kinds of encounters) that I decided I needed to tackle it with my therapist.

His response was, "You can't get much dumber than that. A, you could get shot. B, you could get beat up. Or C, you could get arrested and wind up on the five o'clock news. Tell me, how do any of those outcomes match up with what you want out of life?"

Well, they had nothing to do with what I wanted out of life. They were just adrenalized moments of regression and idiocy—the kind of violent encounters I'd had throughout my life.

We spent a little time on it, and it hit home with me how high risk that behavior was at that particular moment. For the first time I really saw that I was risking losing everything—the love of my life, the family she'd given me, and all the things that had come to me through hard work, including my reputation and potentially even my freedom if I ever got thrown in jail—because I just loved anger too much. That's when I chose to do the necessary introspection and put that beast down for good. I haven't beaten anyone up since. I've wanted to a few times, maybe more than a few, but I don't do it.

When Is It Time to Stop Making Excuses and Do the Work?

For me, it was facing the fact I had to get control of a dark side of my personality that I actually enjoyed but had to deal with because I knew it could ruin my life. And this time I don't mean chemical dependence—unless you count endorphins, because I was addicted to rage and violence.

I know this probably sounds weird to you. It does to most people, but as the kids say, "If you know, you know." Anger has always given me a rush. I enjoy it. It releases a lot of feel-good chemicals in my brain that make me feel happy and alive. That started early, with the gang fights when I was a kid, but I didn't outgrow it. On the contrary, I just got better at finding opportunities to enjoy it. Road rage was a real turn-on. If someone cut me off—or, worse yet, flipped me off—on the road, the way I saw it was that that guy had a beatdown coming, and I was going to give it to them if I had to follow them all the way home and into their driveway to deliver it. It didn't seem like a problem to me. It seemed like a pleasant outlet for my feelings, the way golf or bowling seems to other people.

Now, I go home, I cuddle with my cat, and I cuddle with my wife. It's a good life, and I'm happier than I've ever been. If you'd have told me a few years ago that I'd get to a point where that would be more than enough for me, I'd have laughed at you. Now I can laugh at myself. A few weeks ago, some guys did nearly the same thing to me on that same road. My first thought was whether I should make an exception and go after these two little thugs. And when I got to my exit, I literally laughed at myself and went, "Well, I guess we're not doing that anymore. Let's go home."

What Do You Have to Lose?

Maybe you've got some demons in your closet, ones you let out to play occasionally. Maybe you've gotten really good at keeping that closet locked and barricaded, but it's eating up a lot of your emotional bandwidth to do that, so you're not available for other things like being present for your family. That's true of a few of us and a big reason that many people get chemically dependent.

Or maybe you've had some rough patches in your life that left you bruised or angry or fearful in ways that are blocking your progress to this day. Most people have. Maybe you fall back on some old patterns of behavior you've outgrown but don't know how to shake. You're stuck, and you're tired of playing out the same frustrating scenario over and over. How do you get off the merry-go-round and take control?

Take a look—do some introspection. You've got goals you're not hitting. Why? What's holding you back? I promise that until you are brave enough to dig deep and figure it out, you'll never hit them. Because it's not always about what you have to lose; sometimes it's about what you'll fail to gain if you don't get control and stop letting your fears or your anger, or whatever negative stuff drives you, do the driving.

HERE'S THE DEAL: YOU CAN DO IT, BUT YOU HAVE TO HAVE A PLAN, AND YOU HAVE TO COMMIT TO THE PLAN.

How many people reading this would like to enhance their financial security? Maybe everyone, apart from Elon Musk. Here's the deal: you can do it, but you have to have a plan, and you have to commit to the plan. That plan is probably going to require you to make sacrifices over a long term, because you have to save regularly if you want to build up a nest egg for retirement and security down the line. Are you willing to do that? Are you willing to say to yourself, "I need to cut back because I should be saving 10 percent of my gross," or 5 percent or 25 percent of your gross? The right number depends upon when you want to retire, how much Social Security you'll get at the time, and how much you need to live on, but whatever it is, it requires that you make and stick to a plan. If you make that plan when you're thirty, it's a lot less painful than if you make that plan when you're fifty-five. In either case it's a question of coming to grips with what you want. You know that. Everyone knows that.

So here's the big question: Are you willing to pay a price to get what you want? Everything you get in life comes with a cost. Nothing comes down like manna from heaven. It all takes you doing something. It all takes you committing to something. Most of all, it all takes you being able to see clearly what's going on around you and how you're reacting to it. The sad fact is that most people aren't willing or able to make financial plans and stick with them when it comes to achieving a future goal. And that's why so many older people are finding themselves hard up when they should be able to relax.

I've been in business a long time and seen all kinds of booms and busts in the market. The booms were fun, the busts not so much. They require making tough choices, the kinds that mean people lose their jobs and others lose privileges they've taken for granted. Cuts have to be made, offices have to close, and lives have to be disrupted.

When those kinds of times hit, my people and I face the same kinds of questions you do when you hit the rocks financially. How are you going to make the house payment? What can you cut back on? Sometimes there are no good answers, but you have to come up with them the same way we do. Whatever the challenge is, it forces you to look at the hard facts and to tell yourself the truth, no matter where it leads.

Where Am I Now? What Do I Want? How Can I Get It?

When we've hit those financial rapids, I had a whole list of questions I had to ask myself. Do we need to fix the business? No, the basic business model doesn't need to be changed dramatically, but there needs to be some more introspection on what we charge people and what services we provide. Where can we make cuts on our outlay and increase our input? Those are the questions that have to be addressed when you've got fourteen hundred salespeople and forty-eight offices, but they're really no different when you're dealing with two kids and your house in the suburbs. You still have to figure out what it will take to make it work.

The problem gets intractable though, because so often people know what they have to do to solve it but can't or won't do it. Think about someone with a gambling problem. They know they've got one. They know, too, that there's only one solution to having a gambling problem, which is to quit gambling. They're going broke, their family is going to wind up homeless, and they've got to stop going to the casino.

But they don't. Why is that?

I think it comes back down to what you really want—not what you think you should want and not what your spouse or parents or boss wants. What *you* want, in your heart of hearts. And if you've got a gambling habit, what you want is to gamble. You might really want to change your lifestyle and shake that addiction, but you can't quite come to grips with taking on the behavior necessary to do it. That requires introspection.

The same is true of your financial security. If you've run the numbers and have figured out that you're spending more money than you have, then you've got to come up with a plan that you can live with. Those two things aren't hard to do. The hard part is implementing it and holding yourself accountable because it means changing your habits. And that is where the rubber meets the road, because for many people, spending is an addiction and something that feels good. It doesn't help that our brains aren't really wired to look into the future. We're all about right now. But "right now" is going to suck when you're seventy and have to work the drive-up window at McDonald's.

That's certainly how I feel about exercise. I hate it. But I've made the choice to stick to the program because I'm old enough to see down the pike to old age, and if you're not in good shape, that's a rough and painful road. It may not help me to live longer, but it may help me live better. I know what I want, and I'm willing to do what I have to do to get there. The knowing is good. The doing is better.

Why People Fail

Most people have a dream but fail to do the everyday things that accomplish that, whether that's working out or making phone calls or losing the Starbucks coffee habit and putting retirement money aside. A lot of that comes from their inability to articulate clearly what they do want or selling themselves short of what their potential is. So many people don't reach their potential—not because they're slugs or they're dumb but because they don't even know what they want. It's not as easy to achieve something if you don't know what the thing is.

I have salespeople who make $80,000 a year and are as happy as can be because that's what they need to live well by their standards and keep their lives in balance. That is success for them. I also have sales executives who make $250,000 a year, who either say it's not enough or whine about how hard real estate is. I get sick of the whining. I recently told a salesperson that maybe she should get a different job, and her response was, "Yes, but where else would I make this kind of money?"

Okay, so we'd established what she really valued, which was the great money. Fair enough! Now she needed to change her attitude about the work that let her get that money, and that attitude adjustment started with her changing her self-talk. Taking responsibility for changing her attitude was necessary because it wasn't the work but her attitude toward the work that was the problem. All jobs have their downsides—but hers came with a big upside, which was the money she wanted, so she had to break some bad habits if happiness was her goal. For her that meant getting up in the morning and starting her day being grateful. Going through her morning routine, instead of griping about how rough it was, she needed to practice gratitude for having all she had.

Be glad you woke up healthy and comfortable. Look forward to what the day has to offer, instead of starting out with dread and loathing. I can't remember a day in years that I didn't start out to work saying, "This is going to be a good day." I don't always feel that way when I'm down in the basement exercising. And I don't always feel that way when my alarm clock goes off. But the habit of gratitude kicks in, and I'm glad I'm going to work. I can't wait to see what's going to happen. Might be a good day, might be a crazy day, but at least it's another day.

I wasn't always such a little beam of sunshine. Twenty years ago, I didn't have the mindset and the habits I have now. When I went home from work, my mind was still at the office. I couldn't let go. Now, I go into my house, and I turn that part of my brain off. I rub noses with my kitty, and we sit on the couch. I kiss my wife, and we have some dinner.

Before therapy, I wasn't happy. I didn't tell myself to be happy. I didn't tell myself, "Okay, you did it today. Way to go. Let's do the next thing. Let's read a book. Let's listen to music. Let's pet the kitty." These days, that's what goes down no matter what kind of day I had—good, bad, or in between.

I'm in a totally different place. Whatever issues I've got at work are left at the office. I'll have to face them the next day, but not now. This time is mine. I didn't used to be able to turn things off.

Everybody has to have something, some source of joy that lets them turn it off. Sometimes your kids can do it for you. Your life partner may be that person. You can say a prayer if you're inclined that way. The happiest people I know are the ones who have their priorities in order, are grateful for the good stuff that comes their way, and are secure in knowing what makes them happy. I've got a kid selling houses and making seven figures a year, but the thing that makes him the happiest is his baby girl. He's prouder of her than he is of being this tremendous success story in our business.

And that's why he's a success; he's a happy man, living a life in balance. He's not conflicted, he's not fighting something inside of himself, he knows what he wants and what he values, and he's happy to work hard to get the money to support his family the way he wants to. And when he goes home, he is 100 percent there. He never stops being grateful for what he has.

We still live in the greatest country in the world, one that offers tremendous opportunity. We have a lot of people in the United States who feel put upon or feel that they didn't have a fair shot, maybe because they grew up in a bad neighborhood. Everyone can turn and point the finger at something or someone that messed them up or pulled them down—everyone. But guess what? That moves you exactly nowhere. In fact, it just adds to your feeling that you're not in control of your own life, that you're a victim. Is that a happy state of mind? No, it's not. Is that thinking going to get you from where you are to where you want to go? Very unlikely.

Again, it isn't necessary for you to aspire to something significant by worldly standards. You don't have to make millions or cure cancer or walk on Mars. You just have to figure out what you're willing to work for—what matters to you—and do it. Commit to it and have a plan to get there. Commit to being happy.

> **GET IN TOUCH WITH YOURSELF. YOU MIGHT HAVE TO MOW THROUGH A THICKET OF WEEDS TO GET THERE, BUT IT'S WORTH THE EFFORT.**

External stuff—small stuff mostly—will pull you off course. Other people's opinions about what you ought to be doing to achieve happiness, for instance. But you've got to tune that out.

Separate your ideas of what should make you happy and what you've been told you have to achieve in order to be happy from what you really want. How? Introspection. The answers are in you, not in this book, not in what your parents said, not in what you see on TV. Do the work. Get in touch with yourself. You might have to mow through a thicket of weeds to get there, but it's worth the effort. It puts you back in the driver's seat of your life.

Keep Yourself on Track

It's one thing to say, "Be positive," but in practice we tend to revert to our habitual ways of thinking and acting, so it's good to have reminders around you that can pull you back on course. For me, it takes having a couple of printed cards in front of me on the cover of a file where I keep stuff that I need to look at daily.

These two cards are affirmation cards, and they're probably about thirty years old at this point. The first affirmation card says, "Avoid being sarcastic, impatient, angry; strive to be calm, positive, balanced, enthusiastic, and honest with myself." If I'm not on it and I feel myself backsliding, I read that card and get it back in my head. I've probably read it five thousand times, but I still sometimes need to be reminded.

The second card says, "I'm okay with who I am. I'm going to enjoy today for what it is, the chance to live life to its fullest. And I will take time to enjoy all it has to offer." As I said, I've been reading these daily for thirty years, and the affirmations, as simple as they are, have helped me make myself over as a positive person, one who chooses happiness over anger or bitterness. Old Pissed-Off John will always be inside of me somewhere, I guess, but New, Optimistic John is who I am and how I am in the world. New John is winning because I like him better and because I feed him with affirmative thoughts and actions. I was a negative guy for so long, and my behaviors reinforced that and created habits around how I saw the world and my place in it that just didn't support my happiness. When I first started using these cards to course correct, I sometimes had to read them several times in a day, particularly when I was experiencing reverses at work or in my personal life. But now that I'm happy, I'm more confident that whatever gets thrown at me, I can handle. Things go up, and things go down; I'll figure it out, because I always have.

The more you know about yourself and what makes you tick, the less likely you are to fall back on old, negative behaviors and attitudes that hold you back, and the more likely you are to move confidently toward having the happiness you want.

One of the issues I used to have was how I responded to criticism, especially coming from someone a rung or a few rungs beneath me in the office hierarchy. The outcome of that was that people were hesitant to offer criticism, which was sensible on their parts but lousy for me, in terms of my growth as a leader. If people don't feel safe to say that what you're doing offends them, or hurts their feelings, or makes them feel unvalued, you won't know what you're doing wrong. But you will lose good employees, especially in a competitive market, because they'll go work somewhere else where they feel respected.

Recently at a big meeting of about forty of our sales team leaders, I heard that some people there felt I was being dismissive about some of their concerns, and they felt disrespected. As soon as I heard that, I got them all together and apologized for having made them feel that way and said that I'd been wrong to do so. Without them, I can't hope to stay the top broker in the Twin Cities, and we needed to work together and figure out how to make us all comfortable with how business was conducted. Then I asked if anyone had anything else they wanted to bring up in terms of stuff I was doing that they didn't like, and, to my surprise, a woman spoke up and said she didn't care for the tone of some of the jokes I told or the remarks I made. She didn't find them funny; she found them crass and offensive, and she wanted me to stop telling them. She's a very devout person and didn't want to have to hear that stuff at work.

What was my response? I thanked her for being so honest with me, told her how much I respected her, and promised to break that habit right away. I myself am not religious, but I have to respect other people's feelings, and again, I want to let my team know that their input is valuable to me, that I take them seriously, and that they should feel free to tell me anything, any time. I was grateful that she felt safe enough to say that in front of a room full of colleagues, and I hope my response will encourage others to be honest with me.

Old John's response would have been shorter, a lot more pungent, and not remotely respectful. I'm really glad he wasn't there. But the fact is I'd worked with this person for many years, and I had to ask myself how it could be that I'd overlooked her response to my jokes all that time. Why didn't I pick up on it without being told?

For me, the work goes on, because I have an ego, and sometimes criticism sticks in my craw. But I know it's good for me. So I say the Serenity Prayer to myself, and I take it in and try to turn it into forward movement. I ask myself, "What's best for the company?"

My new, improved self replies, "Well, maybe this time it's best for the company if you shut up, John."

Okay, then!

What's good for the company is what's good for me in the long run, because I've poured a lot of my life into building it into the success it is today, and it would hurt me to see it damaged because I couldn't find it in me to keep myself in line. That's not to say I couldn't be happy without it. But since I am here, I have to make sure that I'm treating people better than I used to, and there's always room for improvement.

The Excuse Trap

When something's wrong in our lives, it's all too easy to look around and find a reason—a reason that conveniently lets us off the hook for why things are screwed up. I've heard this one a few times: "I'm unhappy because my job sucks."

Well, if you can't be happy with the job you have and you want to be happy, then go and get a better, different job. You either have to learn to live within this framework of what you do and be able to separate your home life from it or change what you do, because everybody's job is hard. Everybody has bad days at work. Every one of us is going to occasionally come up against jerks. There's no job in the world, except maybe a lighthouse keeper, that you're not going to have to interact with irritating people or have unsatisfactory interchanges, and you have to accept that as part of the good/bad yin/yang way that life goes and move past it.

Sometimes when I head home at night, I'm not always happy with being the broker at RE/MAX Results. Some days I've had it. But I'm never unhappy at 8:30 the next morning going to work; I'm always happy. I'm always looking forward to it. I'm always feeling good about who we are, where we're going, what today has in store. That's because I've learned to go home and let it go. It may sound dorky, but once I see my cat, that lousy day is over, and it's all joy. I'm on a different page. I'm John from Maple Grove, not John the RE/MAX broker. That's everything, because the next day when I put my John the RE/MAX broker hat back on, I have to be refreshed and optimistic and give it another try. That's a conscious choice I make, to be refreshed and optimistic and not to drag that muck back to work the next day.

When somebody does something to you, that's difficult. You can turn it into an excuse about why you are the way you are, or you can deal with it. And by dealing with it, I mean you have to forgive them. Ultimately, that's how I was able to shake off my anger. I forgave my dad: "I'm done. You're not going to control my life anymore. The fact that you and I didn't always get along isn't going to steal the happiness I get rubbing noses with my kitty. I'm choosing to be happy. And bless you, half of what your life was like was pretty good. And the other half sucked. I can't go back and change it, but what I can do is let it go." That's part of the Serenity Prayer—if you can't fix it, let it go. And that's pretty powerful. Let it go. I cannot change anything about my past with my father. I cannot fix him. I cannot reinterpret it. I can't look at it in a different way and make it all right, but I can choose to let it go.

If your past history is something you regularly fall back on to use as fodder for excuses, maybe you need to do some digging. Therapy is a good place to do it, because a good therapist won't let you fall back on excuses but will push you to come out from behind them and face what's blocking you right now. However you choose to do your necessary introspection, with or without help, you've got to be willing to dig deep and to forgive those who wronged you in the past. Not always because they deserve forgiveness but because you need to shed the weight of the anger you carry. It's not doing them any harm, and it's not doing you any good.

It's a funny thing: despite all the difficulties I had with my dad, I have a picture of him on my desk in his Marine Corps uniform from WWII. He's about twenty, and he looks exactly like I did at that age. I never saw any resemblance between us when I was younger, but we could have passed for twins.

Work on It

The real issue with excuses isn't the buck passing. It's the fact that when we make them, we're not being honest with ourselves. If I know I need to make fifty calls this week to find new buyers, making excuses isn't going to change the fact that I won't have any sales if I don't make the calls. But stuff comes up, and people find ways to turn that stuff into excuses for why they didn't do the legwork. My dog got sick, my parents are visiting, etc. Life is full of distractions, but at the end of the day, if you don't make the calls, for whatever reasons, you don't make the sales. Who are you helping with your excuses? They don't really get you off the hook when you fail. There's no profit in them.

When you find yourself making excuses for not getting done what needed to get done and it becomes a problem in your life (and it will, sooner or later), that's a cue that it's a good time to do some of the introspection I've been talking about. Ask yourself some questions:

- What's my fallback excuse when I fail to follow through with what I need to get done?
- Who or what am I blaming most often for keeping me from getting things done?
- Is there something I can do to eliminate that issue or demand on my time, or work around it, that I'm not choosing to do?
- What am I avoiding? Why am I avoiding it?
- What do I want? What do I need? How am I doing?
- What would free me up to be happier, more in control, and getting what I need?
- How's my attitude on a day-to-day basis?

To the Point

- Take a few minutes and write down some points about what your very best self could be, if you were unconstrained.
- What are the differences between that person you imagine and the person you are today?
- What excuses do you make to yourself when you consider those differences and why they exist?
- What are the traits you like least about yourself? Are you a pessimist? Sarcastic? Withdrawn? Dishonest with yourself or others? We all have characteristics we don't like to look at,

ones we may pretend don't exist or hope others don't spot. But knowing what they are and accepting that they're in you is a part of the introspection you need to do. Identify them, in simple, honest language.

- Try my reminder practice. Write out positive affirmations about what attitudes or emotional habits you're going to change and put them where you will read them at least once a day. If you keep a date book, tape them to the cover. If you work on a computer, make them your home screen. But make sure you read them thoughtfully and with your full attention every day.

- Take positive action that matches the affirmation. If you are in the habit of pessimism, break it by consciously adopting optimism in its place. You might feel goofy saying, "I'm glad to be alive," or "I'm excited to see what today is going to bring," as opposed to your usual negative self-talk, but I promise you it becomes second nature if you do it, and that the language you adopt will actually change the way you look at your life.

CHAPTER FIVE

Deal with It

Savannah was a superstar at our company—so much so that you'd never have suspected she was a kind of human time bomb, and the clock was ticking. She'd put everything she'd had into getting away from where she'd started, adding glossy layers to her presentation to paper over her unhappy past. But you can't outrun yourself forever. I'm not sure what triggered her meltdown—probably just the stress of keeping up her flawless, Energizer Bunny, can-do persona. Cracks started to show. First, she packed on a lot of weight, as eating issues she'd previously kept a lid on spiraled out of control. Subsequently, she became phobic, to the point where she couldn't even leave her

house. Now she was running out of money, but she was unable to work because, between her weight and her fears, she'd become her own prisoner. That's when I went to see her to try and talk her into taking steps toward getting better.

Sometimes when you reach out to people who are struggling, they're still well enough—or have enough self-preservation instinct left—to grab the hand you offer and begin to pull themselves up. Other times, they tell you to go to hell. Fortunately, Savannah agreed to go into therapy and is starting to get her life back. It takes time, but she's moving forward and heading in a better direction. And the key to that for her is that she's finally dealing with all the bullshit she had to process as a child growing up in a profoundly dysfunctional family, where she was given the impossible job of peacemaker between her warring parents and siblings. She's got a ways to go, but the more she uncovers and processes, the more control she's getting back.

None of us gets to pick our families. Some people win the lottery and come from stable, safe backgrounds, but a lot of us don't. We're abused, or we're witnesses to others' abuse. We experience things kids really shouldn't see, much less be part of. It messes us up more than we know, because we don't want to look at it; we want to get as far from it as we can. We find different ways to shove all that ugly stuff down under the water. For me, it was drinking and fighting that let me release the rage that lurked in me. For Savannah, it was food and hiding out. Both were unsustainable and dangerous alternatives to doing the work and dealing with our issues.

Some of us find ways to channel a lot of that submerged anger into being aggressive in business and become heads of industry or politicians, but inevitably the stuff we're avoiding comes back to bite us, our little coping mechanisms fail, and suddenly we're staring into the abyss. If we're able and willing to get help, we can grab our lives back. If we keep walking away from our problems, sooner or later we hit a wall, and there's no more room to run. That's where Savannah was. It's not a good place to be. But how do you climb out of it?

First, This Is Not a DIY Project

Nobody—*nobody*—wants to admit they're underwater and they can't save themselves. It's frightening, because admitting it feels like you're inviting all that stuff you've been pushing away into your living room. But if you're going to deal with your problems in any substantive, productive way, it starts with admitting to them.

First, you need to know what your issue is. Is it really your problem, or are you dealing with someone else's issues that have somehow become your issues? Some people take on others' loads, but that's no way to help them. If, for instance, you're the one taking abuse in an abusive relationship, or trying to keep an addict in your life from using, these are unhealthy and unhelpful ways to live, and you need to take a giant step away. You might need therapy to help you do that, or support from a group like Al-Anon, but it's doable, and it starts with letting go and putting the responsibility for their behavior back on the person who's screwing up.

Sometimes people don't seek help because they don't have a healthy sense of their self-worth. Sometimes they don't seek help because deep inside they feel that they're so irredeemably broken that they can't be fixed. Please, don't think you can't get to the point where you can handle your issues—you can. It will probably take therapy, which a lot of us don't want to admit we need, but we do. It will take focus; you can't deflect and dance around the bad stuff indefinitely, and just burying it will come back to bite you, like it did for Savannah.

What are your issues—the ones you'd most prefer to just ignore or pretend aren't there? Are you angry? Self-destructive? Hurting the people who care about you? Doing things that undermine your life? Know this: you can change. With help, with effort, by dealing with your issues instead of shoving them down, you can change. There's no shame in getting help.

FACE IT—UNTIL YOU GET RIGHT WITHIN YOURSELF, YOU CAN'T REALLY GET RIGHT WITH ANYONE ELSE.

I'm so different from what I was twenty-five years ago that I can't put it into words! I wasn't happy twenty-five years ago. I had money. I had a successful business. I looked like I was making it, but inside I was struggling because I didn't know who I was or what I wanted, and I was just going through the motions. I'd go home at night and think, "This sucks." And the only reason it sucked is because I made it suck. John hadn't yet moved on. John hadn't yet forgiven those in his past. And John hadn't yet "dealt with it."

I started seeing a therapist, and he told me, "Well, you're suffering from depression. You should take medication."

That went on for about a year. And then one day I went to see him, and I said, "You know, I think I'm depressed!"

He looked at me deadpan. "No shit!"

That's just how I was. I wouldn't accept that I couldn't control my feelings and thoughts, I couldn't accept the idea that my brain had a chemical imbalance that caused me to be depressed, and I wouldn't deal with it. I wouldn't take the meds, so I stayed nuts. There was no happiness, no peace, no joy; it was just existence with nothing good coming out of it.

Face it—until you get right within yourself, you can't really get right with anyone else.

The Most Important Step? Forgive Those Who Hurt You.

Because that's essential to healing. Until you can let go of that anger and hurt and resentment, you're going to have to carry it on your back, and that weighs you down, not the people you're mad at. Many people grew up in families that were dysfunctional. Some of us are chemically dependent, some are not, but pretty much all of us have issues. And the more dysfunctional your family was, the more difficulty you're going to have accepting it, forgiving them, and then learning how to live more happily. My dad was a good person at heart; he had a hell of a work ethic, and I got that from him. But he couldn't express affection to me and couldn't deal with his own demons, so that part of him was just lost to me. But part of healing was forgiving him for the harm he caused and getting on with my life. Until I could do that, I couldn't move on. Forgiveness isn't a gift you give to those who hurt you. It's a gift you give yourself, the key out of the cage you're in. It's how you get back your sense of agency.

Who do you blame? Who are you angry at? What were you put through that you didn't deserve, couldn't control, and couldn't escape as a kid? Pull that stuff out and look at it hard—preferably with the help of a therapist—and acknowledge the damage, cry over it if you need to, and ultimately move on. You're bigger and stronger than your past. You just need to learn to put it where it belongs, let go of it, and keep moving. That doesn't happen without forgiveness.

Your Self-Talk Can Help or Hurt You

In an earlier chapter, I talked a little about the importance of the messages we give ourselves throughout the day via our self-talk.

What do you hear when you listen to yourself? Is it negative—"God, I'm so stupid; I can't believe I screwed that up," or "I never can catch a break"—messaging? Usually, those messages are ones we soaked in when we were kids, messages about how we're trash, or dumb, or ugly, or unlovable, or cursed, or whatever. But you're not stuck on those messages. Once you acknowledge they're in your head and begin to really hear them, you can start to unwind them, figure out where they came from. Then you can change up the tape and replace them with positive messages that will calm you, cheer you, and ultimately make a believer out of you in your own potential to heal.

Even if you can't do more, you can start to get yourself into the gratitude habit. Believe it or not, that's a game changer because, as I've said, so much of our attitude toward life and the feelings we have starts with being aware of and grateful for just being alive—the small pleasures, the sunny day, the cup of coffee, or whatever. You're alive and reasonably healthy? You don't live in a box under the overpass? Congrats, you're already way ahead of a lot of people. Acknowledge that every day and be grateful.

Stop berating yourself when you mess up, and start being on your side when you make a good choice. Be the upbeat coach you could have used as a kid to your adult self. Even if it sounds goofy in your head, keep up the positivity and the gratitude, and it will start to come naturally. Little by little, you'll get in the habit of catching yourself when you go negative and turning it around. And your happiness and peace will grow. I'm not saying it will happen overnight. Those messages in your head have been there a long time and have their roots planted in your past. If you haven't had many positive life experiences, internalizing positive vibes, positive thoughts, and positive actions, it ain't that easy to turn your talk around, but it can be done. That's why you read self-help books. That's why you listen to tapes that guide you through meditations. That's why you go to coaching seminars. That may even be why you go to church. Everybody has different places they go to get their direction and support. Find those positive inputs and turn your attention toward them. Tell your inner critic to shut up.

When It's More Than an Attitude Problem

I grew up with a guy who also became an alcoholic and subsequently got sober around the same time I did. We caught up with each other when we'd both joined AA, and that gave us a new rapport and a reason to renew our acquaintance. He was doing well, working hard to provide a more comfortable life for himself than he'd had growing up. At first, he worked in the corporate world, but he'd started going to church again and ended up working for the diocese. It was a good fit for him, but even so, at some point the negativity in his background began to work on him. He lost his job and had to sell his house. He wasn't drinking, but he was clinically depressed.

Alcoholism and depression can be very closely linked, as I knew from my own experiences. Like me, he had a lot of bad stuff rattling around in his head, and his issues were winning. Sobriety is a great thing, but it doesn't cure all your ills. It does make it possible for you to face them and deal with them, though. When you start going to group, you begin to reclaim your life, one day at a time. I sure felt a lot better when I got sober, just like my friend did, but I didn't lose my anger management problem and I still had to do the work—to deal with it—when I got sober.

This guy knew he had problems, but it was hard for him to admit he couldn't fix them, even though AA tells us there are things we can't fix. But he had to come close to losing everything to admit to himself that his problems ran deeper than just quitting drinking could fix. He had to do the work. He had to deal with it.

How Will You Deal with It?

There are many ways to deal with underlying issues that are holding you back. A good analogy is how you'd deal with being overweight, presuming you wanted to change that. There is no end of diets, programs, support groups, doctors, books—even phone apps—out there to help you do that. That said, no matter which method you choose, it all boils down to the same thing: limiting your calories (whatever you're calling them) and sticking to the program. You have to eat less, and you have to do that consistently. It's not that complicated. When I was losing weight, shopping was one of the most important things in my life. I knew myself well enough that I could be certain that if, on a Friday visit to the grocery store, I bought a bag of cookies, there was zero chance that there would be a cookie left at noon on Saturday. If I bought two bags, same thing. Why? Because I'm a compulsive, neurotic person with an eating disorder, and I will get up at two o'clock in the morning and go have four cookies. I don't know why, except it's how I'm built. The best way for me to deal with that is to not buy them in the first place.

I don't have anything in my house that I'm compulsive about. The only thing I have around if I want a little snack is a stack of miniature Ritz crackers with peanut butter in the middle. For some reason I can eat eight or ten of them and stop. I depend on my routines—for breakfast I have two hard-boiled eggs, a banana, and a mini can of Coke Zero, and that is every morning, every day, year after year. Some people find the idea of eating the same thing every single day horrifying. But it works for me, it satisfies my appetite, and I can eat it all in the car on my way to work. Even my nutritionist is good with it, though she's not nuts about the Diet Coke stuff. She knows I limit myself to a couple of the tiny cans a day. And you know what I discovered? The less I eat, the less I want to eat. I keep a roasted chicken around, maybe a tomato, and have a slice of each for dinner. That's how I've learned to deal with my weight and keep it at a healthy level.

Clearly, the first thing to do in dealing with whatever your issues are is to get sober/straight. Alcohol can mask things that need to be out in the open and getting dealt with. It can magnify other problems. You can't enjoy mental health while you're chemically dependent. So start there.

But if that's not your problem, or, like my friend, you've already dealt with that, now it's time to do the harder work. If you're serious about it, look at the things in your life that aren't working and get professional help fixing them.

Is your marriage unhappy? Fix it. Get into couples therapy and figure out whether it can be saved. If not, then get out of it. Unhappiness will just hold you both down and back from a more fulfilling life. It's like having a car that's always breaking down—keeping it might seem cheaper, but it costs you as much or more in the long run. A bad marriage is a lot harder on your happiness than a broken-down car.

Are you depressed? Do you suspect you might be? It doesn't just mean feeling down or sad all the time, though that's certainly part of it. It can also manifest itself in rage, in violence, and in uncontrollable anger. That will either ruin your life or get you killed. Depression has cycles, and when you hit the bottom of the trough, it can get very, very dark indeed. Fortunately for those of us with depression, we live in the age of pharmaceutical wonders. Treatment is good; there are all kinds of medications and almost certainly one that will work for you. There's no shame in needing meds. The only shame is knowing that you need them but being stubborn about not getting them because you think it makes you look weak or because you feel like you should be able to fix this yourself. You can't. Acknowledging that and acting to get the help you need take courage but are a lot less scary than watching yourself take a wrecking ball to your life.

I cannot tell you how much therapy changed my life for the better. It saved me, in the most literal way, and made everything I have now possible. I owe all of it to Dr. Mark and, honestly, to my own efforts to get myself in a better place. There are a lot of therapists in the world; there's no reason you can't find one you like and work with him or her. There are times when you're doing that work that you'll feel like quitting. Maybe you don't feel as though you're progressing, or you're tired of talking about the same damn things and your therapist keeps leading you back to it. Don't quit. Remember, on some level your mind is resistant to looking at the root causes of your problems. You've spent years covering them over, coping with them, maybe drugging yourself to mask them. Uncovering them is going to leave you feeling vulnerable, at least for a while. That feels risky, and sometimes we look for ways to avoid it—like feeling bored, or like we're not making progress, so why keep going? Be aware that you'll probably feel that way at some point in the process. Don't let that feeling talk you out of the work you're doing, because that means you're getting close to the tough stuff, and that's why you're in the room.

Deal. With. It.

What Dealing with It Can Fix—and What It Can't

So you're dealing with it. If your problem is chemical dependency—drinking, for instance—you make the decision and go to AA, and you get sober. Will this fix everything wrong with your life?

No, it won't, and AA will tell you so. Stuff you screwed up before you got sober will still be there—broken relationships, lost opportunities, all of it. If your kids hate you, they're not going to suddenly love you. If you got fired from your job, you're not magically getting your job back. It's not going to make the people who wronged you in your life into nicer people or solve those problems your family has. But— and this is big—you can't solve any of these problems unless and until you sober up. Then, once you've made that commitment, you can decide on how you can address them, one by one, and deal with them. The problem with being drunk or high all the time is that you can't think clearly or assess

YOUR LIFE HAS TO CHANGE, AND THE CHANGE STARTS WITH SOBRIETY.

your contributions to causing those problems when you're not thinking clearly. Your life has to change, and the change starts with sobriety. Once you're sober, a lot of things get clear to you. Maybe you realize that the people you were hanging out with, or the places you were going, were contributing nothing positive to your life or happiness. Maybe now, you'll want to move past them, beyond them, and find new friends or places to be, because a lot of things that looked great when you were drunk don't look all that interesting anymore. Who wants to hang out with a bunch of stoners? It's not fun anymore.

Suddenly, you've got more energy and more time on your hands. When I sobered up is when I bought my first little house, all six hundred square feet of it. How small was it? I had to choose between putting a bed or a chest of drawers in the bedroom, because there wasn't room for both. But I poured my time and whatever money I was making into fixing it up and sold it for a profit. I used that money to buy another house, then more houses, got my real estate license, and away I went.

I still had my issues—the anger, mainly, coupled with the depression—but now that I was sober I could address those in a meaningful way, once I understood those feelings weren't going to disappear on their own. At the point where I seemed to have it all—the business, the beautiful wife, the dream house with matching Mercedes in the driveway, the Hawaiian vacations—yet was still miserable, still unsatisfied with my life, is when I decided to do something about it.

I couldn't have done that, and wouldn't have, had I still been drinking. I had the material stuff that meant success to me, but there was still a big gap between me and any sense of real satisfaction in my life.

But I'd come so far that when I realized I needed therapy to move forward, I just went for it. The medications I needed were another story, though. I'd been an addict, and I was spooked about getting on drugs, even though my therapist explained that they would even out my screwy brain chemistry, not get me high. I was gonna gut it out without them. I was going to be the tough guy, the one who could white-knuckle his way past depression without meds. Anyone who needed a crutch like that was a wimp, I thought. I was going to save myself. And I stuck to that, right up to the day I had to admit that I'd lost that battle and wasn't getting any better. At that point, about thirty years ago, I went on medication. I confidently expect to take them every day of my life until I'm in the ground.

Does that make me a weak person? No, because my problems are beyond my control, and I'm strong enough and confident enough to live with that fact. I take drugs for my cholesterol—does that mean I'm weak? It's a medicine that treats a condition, not a lifestyle choice. I know there are people who are fearful that somehow the meds will change them in a way that will make them feel less authentically themselves. Some people are embarrassed because it seems like an admission that they're crazy or they can't handle their problems. Maybe that's mostly a male thing; we don't like the idea of not being able to do these things on our own. But seriously, that's a childish attitude, like a kid who stubbornly does something after his parents tell him he'll get hurt doing it—then *boom*. Sometimes we're just scared to rock the boat. Maybe things could get worse if we change.

But how many moments of happiness are you passing up in your life because you're just not able to enjoy them? How many compromises are you making with yourself because you know you're not where you need to be in your behavior or your thinking? Is that how you want to live the rest of your life? You only get one, you know. Will you let your pride or fear, or whatever is stopping you, keep you from loving your life? I really hope not.

I'm more awake to joy and happiness now than I ever was. If I could have looked forward at twenty-five and seen where I am now, in terms of how at peace I am inside, I wouldn't have believed it was possible. I love my life. I love my routines. I love my cat, my wife, and my family. I am content. When I get home at night, my cat is waiting for me. We rub noses, and I feed him, then we hang together on the couch and relax. That might sound dorky, but I don't care. It works for me, turns off the workday, and kick-starts my relaxation. I unplug.

You may not be a pet person, but wherever your joy is, you can find it, once you deal with what's stealing your peace.

Work on It

Love it or hate it, we've all got a script in our heads, a script that we hear almost subconsciously when we're challenged or stressed or feeling weak. The script wasn't written by us; it was written for us, by the adults who influenced how we viewed the world and our place in it. Maybe those adults were solid, loving people who bolstered our confidence in ourselves and lifted us up when we were kids. Maybe they weren't, or maybe the messages that stuck with us weren't the positive ones but the negative ones that were mixed in. Whatever they are, you need to separate that script from who you really are, and the first step with that is finding some time and space to really reflect and acknowledge that script and how it makes you feel. Here are some things to think about:

1. When the negative messages start up in your head, whose voices do you hear saying them?
2. What are they saying? Sit down with a pencil and a pad, or your computer, and write them down. What words show up the most often?
3. When does that script play, and how does it influence your response to stress or adversity? Does it make you feel better, or does it make you feel worse? Stronger, or less strong? Motivated or demoralized?
4. If the script you've got isn't working for you, it's time to rewrite it and lose the head trash. Review the statements you've written above. Now revise them to positive affirming statements.
5. Put that list of affirmations somewhere you'll see it every day. Put them on index cards or put them up on the fridge or on your day runner. And every time you see them, read them. Internalize them until the positive messages start to stick. You can train yourself out of negativity, but like any bad habit, it takes being proactive to break and replace with a better one.
6. You've got this.

To the Point

You have nothing to lose and everything to gain by getting better, getting happier, and getting healthier. If you're not happy, if you're bogged down in negativity, stress, or anger, be strong enough to seek out help. Therapy will be one of the best investments you ever make and will pay lifelong dividends.

If you don't connect with the first therapist you meet, find another one. And if you're diagnosed with a treatable illness, take the drugs. Until you feel well, you don't know what wellness feels like. Give it a chance.

And don't try to fix other people. If they stress you, if they make you miserable, let them go. Let go of your anger at them while you're at it, because it's hurting you worse than it's hurting them.

You can't fix the past, but you can leave it behind if you do the work. Deal with it.

CHAPTER SIX

Finding Direction

Once I got sober and saw the world through that very different lens, it quickly became clear to me that I was effectively a blank canvas. I had no idea what life was about, no idea of what I wanted, and no idea how I was supposed to feel. I was just numb. I didn't have any of what I realized should have been normal sensations, which is not surprising given that from the time I was thirteen until I was twenty-three, I was high. My family was clueless, because both my mom and dad were chemically dependent. My sister had never abused drugs or alcohol and had always been the adult of the family trying to keep the family together, and she probably wouldn't have understood what I

was asking her if I'd gone to her for advice. There was no taking the time back that I'd blown through in my early years, but I saw that now it was time to hustle. The first thing I had to do was to get out of my parents' house, but I didn't have any money.

I couldn't find a job, and I didn't have a driver's license because of my DUIs. I used to go down to my friend Steve's house and borrow his work truck to go job hunting because I figured there was less chance of my getting pulled over and arrested for driving without a license if I was driving a work truck during business hours. Steve would come home from work and find me sitting in his living room, because I had nowhere else to go.

Then one day I got a job offer from a community action agency. I told Steve about it when he came home. "These people offered me a job. But listen to this: they offered me $2.32 an hour! How lame is that?"

And my friend Steve, this big, tough construction worker, looked at me and said, "Yeah? How much are you making now?"

Well, nothing.

Point taken. Obviously, something was better than nothing, so I took the job and used it as an opportunity to learn. The agency was involved in energy conservation and helping seniors, and before too long I had studied up on it and was writing their grant proposals. I helped them build out a big energy program for low-income people and seniors, bringing in funds from the federal government. Subsequently, I was hired by the state of Minnesota to write the rules and regulations on the program and to monitor it statewide. Finally, I was making some real money, and I decided to buy my first house, a little rathole in northeast Minneapolis where I grew up. I put my spare time into fixing it up. When it came time to sell it, I decided that if

I was going to make a habit of flipping houses, I should probably get my real estate license.

I continued to do consulting work after I'd gotten the license, but I quickly saw you can't be traveling around doing consulting if you intend to sell houses. I quit the consulting gig and started to learn the real estate business—and it changed my life. I really liked it, so much so that I didn't take a day off for a few years. It wasn't that I was a workaholic; I just loved it, and I had nothing else to do. I was single. I didn't have a particular girlfriend, so all that energy went into my job.

The statistics back then were worse than they are now in terms of how many succeeded in real estate versus those who didn't; over 80 percent of people who got their licenses failed to make a living at it. But in just a few months, I was the third-best agent in my old school real estate office. Honestly, it freaked me out. What in the world were the experienced people doing all day? But there were two older ladies in the office who were aggressive and amazingly effective salespeople, and while I didn't have a mentor in the business, I learned a lot watching their different tactics. Mostly I realized that it was about hard work, and lots of it, and I was fine with that.

This career switch was not greeted with universal joy by my family. My mother was upset that I was leaving what she saw as a cushy government job to sell houses. She cried, but my dad got it. He was a highly educated person, a chemical engineer running a big factory, and by my second year in the business I was earning as much as he was.

But I was happy, because I'd found my way to doing the work I loved—by my direction.

So How Do You Find Direction?

Sometimes you just know what it is you're meant to do. Other times you just fall into it, as I did, and recognize it's the right fit for you. One way to find direction is to do what you love and love what you do. When I'm coaching someone, I don't suggest possible directions to them, because I don't live in their heads, and I don't know what will get their motor running. I can't help people achieve what they want to achieve until they figure out what that is. If I'm sitting across the table from somebody and suggest a career choice that, in my view, would allow them to be the best they've ever been, but they don't see it, it doesn't do any good for me to push that idea, because if they don't connect with it, it's not going to work for them. That's why it's important that people figure themselves out and what they'd like to come next. Even if what they want next turns out not to be the best choice, if it's moving them in the right direction, then I'm satisfied. My role is to help them figure out who they are, what they want, and how to get there from where they are now.

You need to be proactive in the search for the life work that will make you want to go to work every day. One way to do that is to take responsibility for what you spend your time doing and be more aware of how you're using your downtime. What kind of stuff do you do when you're not working? Everything you take in—the television shows you watch, the books you read, the time you spend on the internet—is influencing you and your choices and is going to have some impact on you and where you're going. We know that letting kids play video games for hours every day isn't healthy, that it saps their initiative and stunts their imaginative growth. There's a chance, of course, that one child will use that game time as learning time and grow up to create the kinds of video games other kids will want to play. But if they want to develop other skills, it's not transferable, so there has to be some kind of balance, and staying inside instead of playing outdoors isn't good.

So look honestly at your viewing/playing/reading habits and try to dispassionately assess what it is you're putting into your head. Is it stuff that will somehow push you in a better direction, potentially enlighten or otherwise educate you, make you smarter? Or is it just distraction from reality you fall back on when your workday is done? We have a limited amount of time in life and an even more limited amount of downtime. If you're not using it in some way to move yourself forward, to explore your options, or to learn more about what really interests you, you're not being responsible. Yes, you're entitled to some amount of sheer entertainment, but consuming it all the time is like eating a bag of cookies for dinner.

Sometimes people aren't even aware of how much time they waste on stuff that doesn't help them to advance in any way. But I promise you that unless you intend to maroon yourself on a desert island, watching *Survivor* isn't going to equip you with any useful information. Yet you're investing hours of your time in it or junk like it—time you can't get back.

CHANGING YOUR LIFE FOR THE BETTER, FINDING SUCCESS ON ANY LEVEL, REQUIRES THAT YOU CHANGE THE WAY YOU LOOK AT CHALLENGES AND HOW YOU APPROACH THEM.

Here's a crazy alternative: get into the habit of reading, specifically reading books that apply to your life, what you need, and what you want to accomplish. If you've got a full-time job and two kids to care for, you might have to schedule that reading time for later at night or get up early in the morning. You might have to read on the bus or the train as you go to work. But make that time, create a reading list, and consider jotting down what you glean from what you read, so that it stays with you, and you can put it into context in your own life. Nearly all of the hugely successful people we see changing the world are readers. Many of them, like Elon Musk, have reading lists you can find and follow for yourself. Changing your life for the better, finding success on any level, requires that you change the way you look at challenges and how you approach them. You can learn a lot from people who've already walked your road, because you don't have to make the same errors they made along the way if you know enough to avoid them. That's reason enough to pick up a book right there.

Make a Plan and Follow It

Some people shrug off responsibility for their lives, and often that's because they don't believe they have control over what happens to them. The sense of having agency and responsibility for the choices you make is not necessarily taught well in our schools. We're not really taught the value of a plan or even how to make one to achieve our long-term goals.

When I coach, the action of creating a plan and working it is the toughest challenge to getting people in sales to level up and achieve more. Even when you're talking about helping people get out of being chemically dependent, having a plan is a real benefit to helping them structure their lives after years of chaos. What am I going to do? What do I need to do to get there? And how am I going to stay on top of reaching that goal through the process? Having the plan is the critical first step in accomplishing your goal. The other big piece is accountability. How are you going to hold yourself responsible, and who will you use to help you hold to it?

Does everyone need an accountability partner? Theoretically, no, but I can tell you that for most people I coach it's a huge help. There's a national speaker, named Mike Ferry, who does real estate coaching and has been for as long as I've been in the business. He's got books out based on his program aimed specifically at helping people become their own accountability coaches. One that I read recently is like a day book, with a paragraph every day asking the reader about what they need to do, how they stay in place, and who they need to be to accomplish their goals. It's nothing that hasn't been said a million times before, but when I'm sitting at my desk getting ready for the day ahead and I read a few pages, it perks me up a notch. I'm not a person who's generally in a bad mood or freaked out, but it lifts me, as dorky as it is. Those positive thoughts help reinforce who I am, what I want, and where I'm going—and it's helpful.

Who's Your Accountability Partner Going to Be?

There's no one perfect choice, but who you choose to be your accountability partner matters. It can be a mentor figure who's ahead of you in your career path. It can be a coach you're working with. It can be your significant other or some spiritual figure if you're inclined that way. Who you choose is up to you. But there has to be at least one person, and potentially more than one, with whom you share your plan. You've got to have someone you will check in with, confide in, discuss your progress (or lack of it) with, who will help you be answerable for staying on track.

Whom you choose depends too on what you're trying to accomplish and where you are in life. If you're a high-profile sales executive, you probably have enough money to invest in a coach, and that's a solid choice because an experienced coach has seen other people through this process and is invested in your success. If you're chemically dependent and your plan is getting sober, you have to go to an AA meeting, where you'll get together with someone who's already going down the road you're about to get on and knows what to ask and how to talk to you. Personally, I stayed with AA until I felt reasonably confident in my sobriety and went into therapy with Dr. Mark. He effectively replaced my interaction with my AA group and became someone to whom I was accountable for reporting my progress in dealing with my issues. He retired a few months ago, but we still talk regularly, because there's always room for improvement as my life changes and my priorities shift. We check in quarterly because my biggest issues postsobriety—anger and depression—are largely under control. We've had an ongoing therapeutic relationship for over twenty years, so replacing him wasn't really possible, or even necessary. I haven't beaten anyone up in nine years, so I feel like that demon is pretty well conquered.

What Happens without Accountability?

Too often, nothing good comes from holding the attitude that "I don't need anyone to answer to; I've got this." I think most people do need accountability, because it's so easy to fall out of the habit of following your plan and justifying it to yourself if there's nobody around to call bullshit. That's why you need to be in a group. That's why you need to have a coach. That's why you need to confide in somebody else on what you're trying to accomplish. If you're trying to go from selling ten houses to twenty houses, you need someone to listen to who will give you the good news/bad news truth. Same thing if you're married and the relationship is going south. Boy, you gotta talk to somebody about it, because what you're doing clearly isn't working, and habits in relationships are hard to change.

Now you might be lucky enough to have a friend who's willing to be that person, but honestly they may not have the skill set you need to be there for you in the way you need a partner to be. Their personal involvement with you can be an impediment, too, to having honest dialogue. When you've got a kid who's giving you grief and you're worried about their safety or health because of what you can see they're doing, it's almost impossible for you to handle that well and steer them in a better direction, because you're too deeply involved emotionally. You may come to a point where you hit a wall and need to tell an adult kid to straighten up or move out, but that's a tough conversation for many parents to have, and consequently whatever the behaviors are that the kid is involved in just continue. Not many people are capable of kicking their kid out of the house even when it's clearly justified and maybe the only way to wake them up. These issues can create destructive friction between parents who disagree about the right route to take, and that's no good. It's a tough situation, and you need support from a disinterested person—someone who's not emotionally tied to anyone in your family—to see the issues clearly and to make an effective plan to deal with them.

The First Three Questions

When I meet initially with a coaching client, I have three questions I typically ask them to help me to understand them and to help them better understand themselves:

- Who are you?
- What do you want out of life?
- How are you going to accomplish that?

If their answers to the second and third questions aren't specific, it's important to point that out. Sometimes I get someone whose answer to number two is along the lines of "I want to be a millionaire."

But when I ask them how they intend to make that happen, they're vague or downright clueless. I have to point out that not being able to answer that question with any kind of certainty means that their goal is BS. "I want to be a millionaire." Great. How much money do you have to make to become a millionaire? "Well, a hundred thousand dollars a month." Okay. Well, let's start there. Let's put together a plan based upon what you know, and how to invest money, that will make you a hundred thousand dollars a month. Can you do that? No? Well, then you ain't gonna be a millionaire.

Can you make $10,000 a month? Good. You'll need to save $2,500 of that $10,000 every month. Then, when you get enough money, you buy a fourplex and then you work your ass off for another three years and buy another fourplex. Then, thirty years from now, you're worth $4 million, and your goal is accomplished. But it has to be a goal that's broken down into feasible, realistic steps that will get you from here to where you want to go. Without that step-by-step plan, you're just blowing smoke.

We all know that moving up the corporate ladder is hard. Promotions aren't always based upon who should be next to get a promotion, because the world's not fair. It's just not that easy, but you have to be aware and be focused. And if, after a reasonable period of time, you realize you're not going to get where you want to go working at that particular company, maybe you chose another route, like opening your own store. But that education you got will help you make an informed choice about that too, and if you choose to go work for a place with more opportunity, you take your experience and education with you.

Plans can change. The economy can impact your path toward your goal. Stuff happens, and your plan has to be able to accommodate shifts. Certainly, in real estate we've seen the impact that economic shifts like inflation and interest rates can have on our business. Are we going to go out of business? No. Am I going to jump off a bridge? No. Do we have to be more aware of things like costs? Yes. Now, if the economy goes to hell, more acquisitions will be available to me, and the last time we were in this kind of economy back in '08 and '09, I did really well with acquisitions. So my business plan will likely move in that direction for the duration.

A Plan for Every Season

As we hit our goals, our plans change, and we look for new goals to keep us moving. I've got a plan for myself based on the interests I've got now, things I couldn't have done before I'd met my previous goals for myself. I know I want to work a few more years in my business, although I've largely handed over the day-to-day operational stuff to others. I want to take more time off to spend with my wife and our family. Coaching and speaking to national groups are things I want to do more of, because I find it stimulating.

Most importantly, I want to work more closely with the charitable foundation we've set up. I've seen how well-directed charities can help people to get a leg up in the world, and I'm all in to do that. I see that as my legacy, and as I free up my time, I want to invest it in that effort, along with a significant amount of money to get it on its feet.

America Is Still a Great Place to Succeed

There's a reason that people from countries with little or no opportunity to rise still come here, still struggle to learn the language and get educated, still work two or three jobs to make a better life for themselves and their families. It's all possible here; we see it every day. Regardless of where you're from, what color you are, what your economic background is, wherever you fall into those categories, you can succeed here. Now, if you just got here from Russia, is it gonna be harder than if you grew up in a wealthy suburb? Yep. Does that mean you can't do it? Nope, but it'll be harder. The fewer advantages you have starting out, the more difficult achieving success will be. But there are plenty of success stories about people who rose above the challenges they faced

> **YOU MAY OR MAY NOT HAVE A CLEAR SENSE OF DIRECTION ABOUT WHAT YOU WANT TO ACHIEVE, OR ANYTHING SPECIFIC ENOUGH TO QUALIFY AS A GOAL. DON'T LET THAT STOP YOU.**

because they had a dream and came up with a plan to achieve it. Don't let anyone tell you that you can't. You can.

Work on It

You may or may not have a clear sense of direction about what you want to achieve, or anything specific enough to qualify as a goal. Don't let that stop you. Instead, tune into yourself and do the work to find out who you really are and what interests you and makes you happy, because that self-knowledge will pay off as you move toward finding your direction. Here are some things to consider:

1.   Do you love what you do? Great! If your goal is to do better at it, well enough to meet a financial goal you've set, talk to

some people who are at the level you want to achieve and ask for their advice. How did they get where they are? What challenges did they face getting there? What would they advise you to do? It's amazing how generous successful people often are with their advice when they see someone with real interest and a desire to learn. We all started somewhere, after all, and most of us remember the knocks we took coming up from where we began.

2. Do you hate what you do? Then figure out what's missing in the kind of work you're doing, in terms of what you'd like it to offer that it doesn't. Maybe you like helping people, but the work you do doesn't seem to support that. Maybe you're sorry you didn't follow an inclination you had toward a career earlier in life, and you don't see a way from where you are to where you wanted to be. Consider alternative ways to approach that career, ways to leverage your work experience and education into finding a job in the kind of business you're interested in.

3. When you're in pursuit of a goal, you can't afford to waste valuable downtime consuming junk. Educate yourself. Read books that help you understand your pursuit better or give you valuable insights into developing work habits that will support you and move you forward. Read about people who succeeded in the line that interests you and how they did it.

4. Remember, you have agency. You have the ability to move yourself from where you are to where you want to be. Invest the time into figuring out what your direction should be. Work with a coach or a career counselor or a therapist. Investing in yourself is the best investment you can make.

To the Point

Take yourself seriously or nobody else will. To that end, consider developing the habit of journaling. Make reading lists. Keep track of what you're reading and note what ideas you're getting out of it.

Keep track of what you do with your spare time. How many hours/minutes a day do you spend aimlessly cruising the internet? How many hours do you spend watching TV? If the numbers don't make you proud, put yourself on an intake diet and stick to it.

When you have a clearer idea of your direction, begin to work on a plan that will get you there. Remember, actionable steps, bite-size pieces, and a timetable (even a rough one) need to be part of it. And find an accountability partner to help you stick to it. It will help you over the discouraging moments, support your forward movement, and give you another reason to follow through. Those are all valuable things and can make the difference between success and failure.

CHAPTER SEVEN

Design an Infrastructure of Support

What do you do when you don't know what the rules are, how to behave, or even who to ask? As I said earlier, when I got sober at twenty-three, after ten years of chemical dependency, I was clueless about what normal human feelings were, how people were supposed to comport themselves, or what I needed to learn to get along in regular society.

Granted, it's not everybody's objective to be considered normal, but when I'd been so peculiar in terms of being an outlaw contrarian,

or whatever words you want to use to describe someone rowdy, I was already well behind the normalcy curve. My parents didn't know how to communicate normalcy; it's just what people did, and they didn't see any reason to talk about it. They weren't wired to explain the rules; it just wasn't how they grew up. No role models for normalcy were offered by my friends, who were still living the life I was leaving behind. Now that I was suddenly sober and had my first real job, I didn't have a flipping clue, but I knew I needed to find some insight, fast, and create some kind of structure of support to help me navigate these uncharted waters.

I went to a bunch of different AA meetings and found one I really liked, in the suburb where I grew up. It probably sounds weird, but the atmosphere there was kind of like going to a bar, which was of course my natural habitat. You could pick up women, and everybody was smoking cigarettes. While the stated goal was to help us stay sober, the added attraction was that it felt social and normal for a bunch of recovering barflies. That's where I got my first connection with other people who were trying to lead a positive life. That was my first experience in a situation like that, one where I wasn't in charge, and I didn't know everything. I wasn't trying to start a fight or pick up women. I was just there to shut up and learn. After a while I would share my thoughts if they were relevant. I'd even go out and have a cup of coffee with people after the meeting. I'd never done anything like that, but it's where I found the support I needed. It was a great group. They were the real deal, so that's where I got my toe in the water of trying to have some sort of normalcy in my life. I had to learn how to shut up and listen. But I also had to learn when it was the proper time to contribute. It was my first experience with anything on the planet like that. "Hi, my name's John. I'm an alcoholic." I mean, that's a weird thing to start a meeting out with, but that's what I did.

My first job was my first real exposure to the working world. To my amazement, they didn't think I was a lunatic. They didn't see me as a drunk and a weirdo. In fact, they thought I was clever. I started dating my boss, who was my first actual girlfriend. The other women I'd been with were like me—drunk and out to party, not looking for real relationships. But this girl was smart, college educated, and from a good family in southern Minnesota with a massive cattle ranch. And eventually she said, "I want you to come down and meet my parents."

I totally freaked out. By now I was twenty-four, and I'd never been asked to meet a girl's parents. Never happened when I was a teenager, because their parents told their daughters, "Keep away from him. He's creepy." As we traveled to their home, I can't put into words how unnerved I was by this situation.

Her dad shook my hand, looked me over, and said, "You wanna hop in the truck and take a ride to go look at the cattle?"

Like a doofus, I said, "No thanks," which of course was the biggest insult I could have offered him. Pro tip: never tell a cattle rancher you don't want to go for a ride and look at his cattle. I couldn't have done anything worse. That was immediately clear. I got in my car and drove home, thinking, "How could that have gone so wrong? I can't believe it." Yes, I was sober, I was going to meetings, and I'd even bought my first house, but my people skills were beyond terrible.

My girlfriend forgave me, and we kept going out. Sometime later, she came to see me at my second house and said, "Here's what's gonna happen. Either I'm moving in or we're getting engaged."

And I said, "I don't think so," so that was the end of that relationship. I was unable to move forward. Just didn't have it in me. She was a good person, but that was the end of our relationship.

So by the time I started selling houses, I was very much single, no girlfriend. That didn't mean there might not be some monkey business once in a while, but not that much since I was working seven days a week. I loved selling houses, and I turned out to be good at it, but I was learning on my own, mostly from the self-help books I was reading. Other than AA, there wasn't any real support infrastructure to hang onto in my life.

The truth is I'm not the most outgoing person. I realize it seems preposterous that a salesperson could be as nervous as I was around other people and still succeed. But I was when I was young and showing houses—I'd just sweat right through my suit. I had so much anxiety that I just felt like such a dork. I didn't know what to say. The ability to make easy small talk simply eluded me, though it was obviously something I was going to have to learn to do. I worked at it, and I guess I got better, because I started selling a lot of houses, got promoted, and gradually grew a little bit as a person, feeling more comfortable in my own skin.

How much easier would it have all been if I had had a mentor or someone to ask for advice? I didn't, though. AA was my place to connect with others, and the self-help books provided some useful clues.

Creating Your Own Support System

In coaching people facing the same challenge I experienced—a lack of supportive infrastructure as they try to remake their lives—it's been countless times that I've told somebody, "You need a therapist." For me, going into therapy and finding Dr. Mark provided me with the infrastructure I needed to get away from AA. Twenty-five years later, he retired, but we're still in touch, and I have a regularly scheduled check-in with him.

If you're feeling unmoored and keep coming up against the same old internal obstacles, why are you not in therapy?

If your background/childhood/family life is a road map of dysfunction, why are you not in therapy?

If you can't get out of your own way, why the hell are you not in therapy?

No, it isn't a quick fix. It took a while to make you what you are, and it will take a while to work on yourself and improve. But regular meetings with a therapist can provide you with some of that supportive infrastructure you need to move ahead. Many, many meetings went by as I danced around getting to the point with Dr. Mark, because we don't generally want to look our issues in the face and name them. But I figured out stuff that has made the life I have now possible, and I probably would be dead or in jail by now if I hadn't done so, because I was addicted to anger and adrenalized by violence.

While I'd say it's pointless to try and rewrite the past or to dwell on it too much, it's also true that you don't get anywhere by refusing to acknowledge it, to see it for what it was, and finally let it go. If you don't deal with it, you can't get past it. But once you do, you can move into a bigger, better life that looks ahead, not behind.

It took me a long while to realize that the anger that periodically burst out of me as road rage was tied to my anger at my dad. I had to let it go, and I had to forgive him before I could really grow past that anger. And I didn't manage that until I was sixty. But it's given me a better life, and that better life was worth the work.

It's taken me this long—I'm recently seventy—to be able to take the "Who cares?" attitude that I have now. I can choose to work more or less, have more or fewer cars in my collection, buy a big house or several, or sell them all. Those are choices I can make and that I've earned the right to make. I would not have gotten here without AA and Dr. Mark because, whether it's having coffee with your best friend, working with a therapist, or talking to a religious leader, you have to have someone to talk to who will listen and let you get some of those things out in the open. No, just airing it doesn't fix the problem, whatever it is. But until you admit it's a problem, it ain't getting fixed.

Why do I repeat dangerous or destructive behavior? How can I be a better person to my significant other? That was a mystifying thing for me because it's hard to love somebody when you're not loving yourself. You can't be the right person for someone else when you're not right with yourself. I didn't get wholly well until I finally took Dr. Mark's diagnosis of depression to heart, got on medication, and discovered that I wasn't nearly as angry as I'd been.

Can a Coach Help?

I never had my own private coach. I participated in some group coaching at industry events, but honestly the people running them knew less than I did. I realize that's not the best attitude to bring to the table, but it was mine. I wasn't going to pay someone to tell me how many calls I had to make; I knew that stuff cold. But I've been able to coach a lot of people through difficult passages to success, and that's been an education for me too, because it's helped me to codify my own rules for making success happen.

A good coach is someone who knows what you're up against because he or she has already been there and done that. A great coach brings a skill set to the table—the set you need to hone and adapt to your own situation to find the success you want. And a coach brings accountability, because if you're not putting in the work outside of your coaching sessions, if you're making excuses for yourself instead of implementing changes, or worst of all if you're bullshitting, a coach will call you out on that and push you toward understanding why you're undermining yourself.

How can you create accountability that outlasts your coaching session? I count on to-do lists. Once a week I sit down and make a list. How many calls do I need to make, by when? How many meetings do I need to take? What's my deadline? I've been running my life this way for some twenty years now, and I can tell you that I've never missed my self-imposed deadline for getting those tasks done. In fact, I'm dependably ahead of schedule every week. My assistant, Alicia, sits down with me to help me pull that list together, then she sets up the appointments for me, and I go to those appointments and make my calls.

This takes self-discipline, which a lot of salespeople lack. But it's not a thing for me to say, "I'm not calling them. I'm sick of this." There are plenty of times that I'm making my calls when they're tough to make, but I make the calls. I wasn't born like this; I adopted this behavior until it became second nature. When you're in charge, you have to become your own task master, set up a system that makes sense to you, and stick to it. You have to have a plan, and you have to have a system to implement it. Most people need accountability, and I've helped many people in sales with becoming more accountable. My own accountability is to me: Am I making progress? Am I hitting my goals through my appointments? Do I need to rethink them?

Using Your Life Partner or Peers as Accountability Partners

For a lot of you, your infrastructure is going to include your spouse. That means that your partner needs to understand what it is you do and what kind of support that work is going to require. I've seen marriages or relationships flounder, because one person is taken up with their goal or their work and their significant other starts to feel like, "Well, everything's more important than I am to you. And you never find time for me because you're always hanging out with clients or colleagues or working." Letting them in on a better understanding of what you're doing and why it matters can help both them and you. Talk to them about your plan and what you hope to achieve. Lay out the steps you're taking to implement it. Be honest about what you're messing up on and solicit their ideas for helping you to stick to the plan. Not every relationship works this way, of course, but if you need support and you're getting resentment from your partner, it's probably a good idea to have that conversation and try and defuse it.

Depending on what you do, groups of like-minded peers can also be great accountability partners. I've seen many instances in which somebody goes and listens to a speaker, then joins a coaching group and meets others with whom they can share ideas and ways to do better. If your objective is, for instance, to raise money for a cause, meeting on a regular basis to talk about obstacles you're hitting in your fundraising is guaranteed to get you some good advice and expert insights. And maybe someone there has another problem and you've already cleared that hurdle, so you can help them.

It's the same thing for company events and conventions. I've been with RE/MAX for thirty-six years, and I've been to thirty-five RE/MAX conventions and to at least thirty broker conferences. Most of the time I don't get anything out of it, because most of the time I'm an arrogant SOB. I've got the biggest RE/MAX franchise in the world; what are any of these people going to tell me that I don't already know?

But you know what? I've sat and listened to all kinds of speakers, sometimes being bored, checking my watch—*is this over soon?*—then hearing them put out an idea that I actually scramble to write down, because it's a good one that I hadn't thought of already. The thing is if you listen to someone who's an acknowledged expert for an hour or two, they're going to offer up something you'll find useful, even though you may not be clicking on all cylinders with them. Whether they're talking about what you do and how to do it or what they see coming down the pike in the future, they're going to have a different perspective than yours, and that can be illuminating. There's a guy I know who's a real estate guru and coach and has been since I've been in the business. At an event last year, I picked up a copy of his book and brought it back to my office—and every day I pick it up and read three or four pages. Now, he's not saying anything I haven't heard a hundred times or anything I couldn't have said myself. But even so, when I'm sitting there reading it, thinking about what he's saying and why he's saying it, it works for me because it stimulates my own thinking. I get something out of it that I didn't have, even if that's just a few minutes spent focusing on a specific issue.

I guess the lesson in that is that you're never too smart to learn and never too sophisticated to be surprised by a good old idea reframed in a way that makes it feel fresh.

Be Accountable to Yourself Too

There are going to be times when there's nobody there for you but you, and you may be sorely tempted to mess around and put off the work you need to do, though you know that choice will certainly come back to bite you. That's why I heartily endorse the idea of a weekly task list as I outlined above, which you create and to which you commit yourself to performing by or ahead of deadline.

If your goal is to grow your knowledge, expertise, and understanding of a specific field or skill set, there is nothing better than marshalling your downtime and educating yourself. You're not getting better or smarter or stronger, or anything else worthwhile, if you're not able to hold yourself accountable.

I say this as a guy who knows that, had my trainer not come to my house this morning to work with me, I wouldn't have worked out. I guarantee it. When the alarm goes off at 6:00 a.m., my first thought is to call her and tell her not to come, because getting a couple more hours of sleep sounds great right then. When we're in Arizona, I salve my conscience by going for walks three times a week, but if I don't Zoom with my coach, I don't get the benefit of the exercises she puts me through. Who loses if I get away with that? Me, of course. So I Zoom and roll around on the floor and feel better about myself. But the reason it all works is that it's part of my schedule. It's on the calendar. That's what gets it done. Neither I nor you can count on motivation in the moment to do what we know we need to do. That's why we have to build accountability into our efforts and into our schedules.

What do you do when nobody's watching? Are you cruising the internet, goofing around? Are you watching trash TV? Or do you put your downtime to use to move you forward? There's a reason that the most highly successful and effective people in the world believe in reading and share their booklists with the world. Not surprisingly, a lot of CEOs do the same thing, in private reading groups. These are people who know that downtime can be both pleasurable and useful, and that reading is something even the busiest person can find time for. Want to know about how someone you admire got to where they are in life? Chances are that person has written a book. Want to know more about how successful people got successful in their fields? There are books about that, whether the field is sales, medicine, finance— you name it, there are people in those fields writing books that will teach you more than most college courses, and on your own schedule. I talked about this earlier, but it bears repeating: take yourself seriously if you expect others to do so.

No matter how smart you are or how successful you are, if you want to grow, there's no sense in stopping the learning process. You may have a lot of good insights, but there will always be someone with better ideas, and there's no reason not to explore them. If you don't like reading, you can listen to recorded books, and that's a great way to make your time on the treadmill or on your commute even more productive and pleasant. There are professional groups you can join in most fields to learn from your peers and share ideas while networking. There are online classes available from the most prestigious universities in the country, most of which you can audit for free, in nearly every discipline. You can watch those at your leisure and on your schedule, which probably beats another season of *Real Housewives* in terms of what you learn from it.

Other Ways to Create Supportive Infrastructure

Let's take a moment to review. The first thing you've done toward finding the success you want is taking stock of yourself. Who are you, and what do you really want? The second step is creating a detailed plan that will take you step by step toward that goal. Then, you have to have a system in place that lets you continually review your progress to make sure you're sticking to your plan.

In my company, I meet monthly with my management team to go over the results we're getting from our plan. How are the numbers looking? Are there any issues we need to deal with that are cutting into those numbers? Do we need to bring on more people in specific areas of the business to eliminate a bottleneck, or do we need to make cuts? We've got a plan, and we're working it, making tweaks as the market requires them. Tough questions are asked, and difficult decisions are discussed. When you're working with a team, you all need to be on the same page. You don't have to have the same opinions, and you don't have to agree on the answers to the questions, but you all need to be in pursuit of the common goal and end result.

I love that process of teamwork, and it's probably why I still find the business as intriguing as I do. Teams hold each other accountable and provide support for an ongoing effort—certainly the good and effective ones do. You don't want someone in the outfield watching home runs go by; you want someone who's going to make the catch or at least make the greatest possible effort to do so. Everyone is loyal, everyone's looking to praise effort and results, and everyone wants to motivate their teammates.

That's what it is to be part of a team. We're happy when we win, we're pissed when we lose, and we're going to keep getting better. If you're having troubles, I'm here for you. If you're killing it, I'm loving you. That's what a team is. That's what a loving partnership is, whether it's a marriage or not—understanding that you're individuals, but you're both going in the same direction. Support in a partnership doesn't mean you both have to be in the same business. You just have to be on each other's side.

THE MORE YOU KNOW, THE MORE PROGRESS YOU'RE GOING TO MAKE, AND THE MORE STIMULATING YOU'LL FIND YOUR LIFE.

Support groups can be formed around personal goals or professional goals. Accountability has to be baked into realizing those goals, and that's something a group can supply. Are there other people on your level, colleagues or others who are experiencing the same kinds of issues you are? Maybe they'd like to participate in a group where they could air their thoughts, bring their challenges, and support one another. As long as it's a regularly scheduled meeting and you stick to the business you're there to discuss, this can be a tremendous addition to your support system and to theirs.

Two things that undermine people in their search for supportive infrastructure are insecurity and hubris, either individually or in combination. An insecure person is hesitant to ask for others' opinions or suggestions because they're afraid of looking weak. Someone who's too full of "I won't listen to others," because they imagine they already know it all and don't need to hear anyone else's view. If you're resistant to engaging with others in the pursuit of your goals for either of these reasons, neither fear nor pride is really going to help you as much as putting those things aside will.

The thing is the more you know, the more open you are to learning, whether that's from books, mentors, peers, or coaches. The more you know, the more progress you're going to make, and the more stimulating you'll find your life.

Forward movement is what it's all about. Keep it going.

Work on It

You've made your plan—you've thought it through, made it as granular as you can, and identified the steps you need to follow to accomplish your goal. Now you need to plan out how you're going to find the support that will help keep you on track.

Support comes in a few different flavors, but we can narrow it down to two big categories: people you pay to provide accountability, input, and support; and people who do it for you for free. The advantage of paying someone—a coach, a therapist, a trainer, whoever—is that part of the deal is your payment, and most of us are apt to want to get the good out of the money we spend. In my observation a lot of people join gyms, then don't go after the first few times.

Why? Because there's nobody waiting for them there to encourage them or provide insights on how to work out more effectively. They don't have a standing day and time, and there's no one to report to. People with trainers tend to do better because a relationship develops, you don't want to disappoint the other person, and you put the effort in because someone is there watching and encouraging you, helping you over the tough spots and making adjustments to the program depending on your progress. That's accountability.

A therapist is a great sounding board for people with personal issues holding them back, for many of the same reasons. Again, you've got an expert on your side, someone whose job it is to help you and who has the education and experience to do it. And you've got the accountability piece built in by virtue of taking regular meetings with your therapist and them having the skills to prompt you, move you in the right direction, and call you out on your BS.

A professional coach is someone who's an expert in the area in which you want to grow. They've either been in your business or understand business at a high level and in a way that is applicable to your goals. They will give you direction—make suggestions, assign tasks, or otherwise spell out ways to use your time and efforts in the most productive ways. You will follow their directions and report back. Again, you've got expertise and accountability built into the process. It's a great investment.

On the unpaid side, you've got your life partner, your peers, and groups like AA or professional associations, all of which can be tremendous sources of support. A mentor at work or in a similar business can give you the benefit of her or his expertise and experience and be a sounding board for your goals and ideas. Even just getting together with a friend or peer group can be a great way to create the support you and they need, as long as the meetings are regular and you stick to the program you're there to discuss.

Whatever you decide to do, think of it as an investment. You're less likely to waste your time or spin your wheels when you realize your time and attention are worth something.

To the Point

1. Get into the schedule/list habit. Make this a part of your week, every week. Have time set aside to create your list and commit to accomplishing everything on it by or before the week is up. This helps you schedule your efforts in the most efficient way, shows you where your bottlenecks are, and creates accountability around your tasks. If, for instance, you need to make fifty calls in a week, figure out ahead of time when you'll be doing those calls.

2. Talk to your partner about how you'd like them to support you. Don't turn them into your personal cop but set up some ways in which they can help you get where you want to go.

3. Find a mentor, either at work or elsewhere, who can understand what you're trying to accomplish and share their insights and experience. Many successful people are willing to make time to mentor others, as long as the demands on their time aren't too taxing. Invite that potential mentor to lunch or an early breakfast and ask if they're interested or willing to take you on as a mentee.

4. If you need help with big stuff—if either your issues or chemical dependency are holding you back—seek help from someone who knows how to help you. AA is a great organization with all kinds of meetings for all kinds of people. If you

don't like one meeting, try another. You'll find a place that feels right, and you'll learn from those who've been down the road you're on.

5. If you have other kinds of issues, find a therapist. There are a ton of them out there, and there's going to be someone who's going to be a good match for your ways of communication. Don't get frustrated if you find yourself going over the same material over and over—that's part of the process and has to happen before you hit a breakthrough. Just do your part by keeping it real, not wasting time, and being a working partner in the process of seeking your joy and inner peace. If it can work for me, it can work for anyone.

CHAPTER EIGHT

Answer the Seven Questions

Confession time. When my trainer goes on vacation, which she occasionally does, my accountability goes with her, and I'm about as likely to roll around doing floor exercises at 6:30 a.m. as I am to light my hair on fire. I've been working out for twenty years, and I still hate every minute of it. If my coach doesn't show up, neither do I. It's not that I don't know how to work out, but my inability to bring myself to do it without her holding me to it is why I got a trainer in the first

place. That's the truth, and we always need to tell ourselves the truth if we're going to move forward.

How can you apply the wisdom you glean from your coach to your life or career plans in the most productive way? And how can you impose accountability for yourself in following your plan once you're out of your coaching session? How do you come up with something that works for you and that you're willing to stick with?

I've listened to hundreds of coaches and motivational speakers, many of whom make big bucks doing what they do, but I've observed that their messages don't hit in a meaningful way most of the time for the people they're speaking to. Sure, the ideas can get you fired up, and you may leave the speech or the class thinking you've found the golden key, but that fire burns out fast if you don't also leave with a methodology for keeping it going.

Do you need someone—a group, a coach, a partner—to help you stick with the plan you've designed? There's no right or wrong answer. It really hangs on where you are in your life at this particular time and what the best way is to reliably get the results you want.

So how do you determine what you need and how to get it? Here are the seven things I believe can make the difference between success and failure.

Do You Schedule Your Habits and Behaviors?

Everyone is different. For myself, I don't need anyone to tell me to make the phone calls required by my business. I find a list useful because it keeps me on track with what I know I need to do and the order in which those things need to get done, but the list doesn't "make" me follow it. I follow it because it's helpful. I don't need a coach for that.

Knowing what you need to pencil in time for—scheduling—requires some honest introspection and the ability to determine where you most need to apply yourself. I know that having my coach on my schedule, along with watching my diet, is going to help me maintain my health. I'm not that young, but I'm in as good a shape as I was twenty years ago, because I'm motivated by a desire to live a longer and more functional life. Will it work? I have no idea, but that's my goal.

I also firmly believe that scheduling and routine have innate value in that they support mental health, accomplishment, achievement, and ultimately happiness. I can tell you, too, that I'm not alone in this opinion; you'll find very few good coaches or therapists who will tell you, "Don't worry; you don't need a schedule. Just do whatever you want." Nope—doesn't work. You need time frames; you need to know when to stop one thing and start another. You can't let things drag on or get distracted and drawn away from doing what needs doing now. You have to know when to say, "Okay, I'm done with that—time to move on to the next thing."

If you're a salesperson, you absolutely need to spend a given amount of time working on your business, prospecting, or spending time with your clients. You've got to make calls. You've got to work on your files, and you've got to go out with your buyer or seller. The proportions of your day that you spend on any of these activities need to be figured out and adhered to. How long does it take you to make your phone calls? How many phone calls per week are in your business plan? In real estate as of this writing, listings are worth their weight in gold. If you list a house in a reasonably desirable neighborhood, chances are it will be sold quickly. If you have a buyer, you need to put the time into getting them to look at those listings, because if they're going to write an offer, they're going to have competition and may well have to go in higher than they expected to win. You're likely to spend more time on the transaction because of this since demand is so powerfully outstripping supply. All of these kinds of things have to be factored into balancing your schedule.

How to Build a Schedule That Works

A good schedule supports efficiency and balance in your life—your whole life, not just your work life. Remember that your spouse and your kids come ahead of your job, so when push comes to shove, you've got to allow for that in your schedule, because their time matters too. That means that if, for instance, you have a family, you need to note your events with them in your schedule to avoid conflicts. If your kid has a baseball game, you can tell a client who wants to meet, "Sorry, I'm busy then. Would tomorrow work?" or whatever. Clearly, there might be times when you have to miss that game, but knowing that it's on your schedule helps you not to inadvertently plan something else at the same time.

Schedule time to spend with your partner too, whether that's a dinner out or an afternoon at the driving range, because your partner comes second only to you. What I've found is that if you don't set time aside for the people who matter most, that time gets used up in other ways, and those family or couple activities just don't happen. That's particularly true for a person who's driven, who's constantly looking for a reason to get back to their desk. But if you don't set time aside to spend with your partner and your kids, they'll be unhappy, and you'll be unhappy. Life goes by fast, and you don't want those regrets dogging you.

When I was twenty-eight, this kind of thing meant nothing to me, because I didn't have anyone I cared about. There was an older guy I liked who worked in my office, and I remember him telling me that after you hit fifty, time really starts whipping by. Turns out he was right. That's why you can't get into the habit of putting first things last. I've talked about the importance of being able to say "no" when it's the appropriate response, and that certainly applies to time management.

Every successful salesperson I've ever known or heard of makes their calls religiously every single day, depending on what their market plan requires. So do I, and so must you. No, you're not going to consistently enjoy it. If you're prospecting, you won't be saying, "I can't believe how much fun this is calling 'for sale by owners.' I love it when they hang up on me." But when you call one and they say, "Maybe you should come over," suddenly life's looking better. You don't have anything signed, but you've got an appointment, and you can't get anything until you first get that appointment.

I'm not immune to rejection. Recently, I had five appointments to talk to potential recruits about joining our team, and I was zero for five. I mean, I got dusted. Still, I made the contacts, so who knows? Sometimes being in second place is all you can hope for, and if you get lucky, the brand or the person in first place screws up and then you've got a chance. They'd all worked here at different times and had been recruited away. Despite the turndowns, I put these conversations in the plus category, because I reestablished our relationships. If they become unhappy with where they're at, they know they're wanted here.

Do You Spend Your Time with People Who Support Your Plan/System?

Who are you hanging around with? The people with whom you spend your time can have a bigger impact than you might think on how good you are at following through on your plan. A big mistake salespeople often make is spending too much time hanging out with other salespeople. That gets you nowhere most of the time. I had a big group of guys my age I used to hang out with, but their attitude was so negative about what they did—lots of complaining, not much optimism—that I pulled away from them. Why? They didn't advance my thinking, and I wasn't impacting theirs.

My friend group is small, on purpose. Between family and work, my time is mostly spoken for. But I've got good relationships with several of my employees, relationships that bolster their plans and mine and contribute to collegiality at the office. I've been honored to have been invited to their children's weddings and other big family events, and I value their input and insights.

I've got people in my family that I care about but who I don't spend a lot of time with. It's not because I don't love them; it's just that our lives are so different, and our choices so divergent that we don't have a lot to talk about. We get together for some of the holidays and catch up, and when someone dies in the family we show up and represent.

How Much Time Do You Spend Feeding Bad Habits?

Are those habits undermining your attempt to move forward? One of the most toxic I've seen has to be heading downtown for a few drinks with friends after work or hitting the local bar together as a regular thing. That's not going to support forward movement, because hanging out in bars and drinking don't improve things. It's much more likely to undermine you, negatively impacting your health, energy, and outlook. It's expensive too. If you partake in that kind of socializing regularly, it's certainly going to affect your time management, along with your ability to amass savings. And it's time lost that you could have spent with your family.

What's Your Personal Growth Plan?

Having a solid business plan and working it on a set schedule is mission critical to getting where you want to be professionally. But there's a corollary piece that's just as important in the long run to getting the career you want, and that's becoming the person you need to be to realize your goals and build on them. That piece is your personal growth—your education—and you need to be investing time in it.

When I think back on the way I was educated at home as a kid, there were yawning deficits in what I needed to know versus what my parents taught me. We never talked about how to make money, what the options were for careers, and how someone could prepare for that. We never discussed what to do with money after you'd made it or how people invested and grew their money. Nobody explained about saving for retirement—how much you need and how to put money away to support yourself. These things just didn't come up because it's not how my folks looked at life.

You may have grown up in the same kind of family, which is pretty typical of the way working class people live. Alternatively, you might have gone to college, graduated with a degree, then figured you'd learned all you needed to know to get by. But did you learn all you needed to do better than that? If not, you can make

IT'S WORTH THE COSTS TO MOVE MORE QUICKLY TOWARD YOUR GOALS, SO ASSESS YOUR PROFESSIONAL AND PERSONAL WEAK SPOTS AND LOOK FOR THE HELP AND EDUCATION YOU NEED.

up those deficits as a motivated adult by reading, by taking classes or auditing them online, and by using your downtime productively.

Maybe you need a coach. Maybe you need a therapist. Maybe you need both. It's worth the costs to move more quickly toward your goals, so assess your professional and personal weak spots and look for the help and education you need.

Are You Good with Your Partner and Family?

Ask yourself: What do I need to do to strengthen my relationship with my spouse? How is my family doing? Am I truly present with them when we spend time together, or am I letting other stuff—work stuff, for instance—intrude on our time together? It may sound counterintuitive to suggest that you need to be able to put work aside altogether when the purpose of this is to help you do better in your career, but having healthy boundaries is important, because enhancing your happiness is healthy and supports your mental health and well-being, and family life is a big piece of that.

The flip side is that if you've dutifully spent years visiting with family members whose company makes you miserable, you hereby have my permission to stop. There's no good reason to subject yourself to miserable holidays with people who are toxic, angry, negative, mean-spirited, or otherwise destructive to your peace and happiness. Send flowers if you feel guilty and find something better to do. A frozen turkey pot pie eaten in peace beats a lavish sit-down Thanksgiving dinner mired in conflict. You can quote me on that.

Are You Honest with Yourself?

Getting everything that you want to get out of life requires that you're okay with yourself—and that's not so easy. You have to have a degree of self-awareness and be honest with yourself. When something in your life is not supporting your peace and happiness, you have to be able to say, "This sucks. I don't want to work there. I don't want to live there. I don't want to be there," because it's not wrong to be unhappy. You have to recognize that these events have led to unhappiness. So what do you do? You try to fix it. If you're unhappy, get yourself into therapy. If you and your partner are unhappy, get the both of you into counseling and don't wait for it to fix itself. Ask yourself: Are things better this month than they were last month? If they're not, don't wait it out.

I know couples who sleep on separate floors in their homes because they don't want the kids to know how much they hate each other. If that's what your marriage looks like, you might be better off out of it.

Have You Planned Your Financial Future?

Whether you're single or married, and no matter what age you are, it's not too soon to start planning for your future. Eventually you're going to want to retire, and you can't bank on a lottery win to finance that. You're going to need money in place to pay for your retirement needs, especially if you intend to support any kind of halfway decent lifestyle in retirement.

There are a million books written by financial planners and other experts that can guide you through creating a financial plan that will make that possible. But the time to begin is now because yesterday is already gone. Don't wait for a better time because there won't be one.

Either read some books or work with a financial planner—better yet, do both. It's easier to scrimp and save when you're young and doing with less will incentivize you to work harder now.

If you have a spouse, you both need to talk about this plan. How long do you both intend to work? Can you predict reliably what your earnings will be over the next five, ten, or twenty years? How much do you spend every month now, and how much are you likely to need when you retire? What kinds of fixed expenses will you have in retirement? How much can you put away each month now, and where is the best place to put it? All this belongs in a spreadsheet or on paper, because a plan needs to be written down so that you can hold yourself accountable to follow it.

Get Your Budget On!

Financial planning is a great start, but it's only the beginning. What you have to do to support your plan is to learn to break down your income versus your spending and use those numbers as the basis for a budget. You know how much you bring home per month—that's the starting point. Now, what are your regular expenses—rent or house payment, utilities, car, insurance costs, your weekly food budget—all the little and big things you have to deduct?

Once you've got those down, you know how much you can afford to save. If your plan tells you that in order to meet retirement goals, you need to save more than you do, so you start looking for places to cut spending. Pricy gym? Check out the Y. Are you eating out too often? Try cooking at home and buy food ahead of time that supports that effort. Shop sales and batch cook on a day off so you're not starving when you get home with no recourse but grabbing takeout. Look at what can be let go with minimal pain, then dig deeper. Maybe you have too many streaming channels. Maybe you're paying for magazines or other kinds of subscriptions you don't really use. Maybe you're at Starbucks too often.

Budgeting is hard at first, because it requires you to break habits and to make choices that initially might seem like a drag. But as your nest egg grows, you'll feel better about it. I promise, being thrifty will seem less like an imposition and more like a game you're winning.

If you're married, one of you probably makes or has more money than the other. You both need to be clear on how much you're both making, where it's going, and where it's held, whether that's in investments or at a bank. Don't let your mate tell you they don't want to know, or they trust you to handle it, or anything like that. Everyone needs to be an equal partner in the effort and the information sharing, whether or not they're able to contribute equally.

Work on It

I realize that the steps, above all, require effort on a lot of different levels. But like any big effort, it can be broken down into many smaller bite-sized efforts, which makes the work a lot less intimidating and much more palatable. Here are some things to consider:

- They may require you to do research, for instance, if you're just dipping your toe into planning your personal finances and need to understand what kinds of investments might be suitable for your age and stage of professional life. There are experts everywhere, eager to advise you via books, financial columns in the newspapers, magazines, television, etc. Take the time you need to educate yourself, starting with the vocabulary of financial planning, so that you can understand the recommendations and warnings they may give you. Not all planners are created equal, so don't sign on with anyone you have not personally vetted. If they feel too *sales-y* or like they're pushing you in a direction you're not clear on, find someone else.

- They may require self-work, which means finding a therapist or a coach that you feel good about. Again, this is an area in which you can do your own research very effectively, thanks to the internet. It's also good to solicit recommendations from people whose judgment you trust, if they're willing to share that information. You can usually meet with a coach or a therapist once to see if your goals align with what they do. These kinds of experts usually have specific areas of expertise, so work with those whose expertise matches your needs.

- They may require you to pursue more education and/or networking opportunities. If you are in a profession, you should probably check out whatever professional organizations there are in your field. These are often a great place to learn from more seasoned people in your business, to connect with coaches or mentors, and to interact with your peers. It's a good idea to ask people who've been doing what you do for longer than you have and ask their advice before investing in a class or any other kind of professional development. What would they recommend? What would they avoid? Not every conference or meeting you attend is going to pay off, but if you're paying attention and using the opportunity to meet others in your field, you're likely to walk away better informed than you came.

To the Point

Why the seven questions? Because they all point to one very important fact: your agency, your ability to make powerful choices around your career and your wellness and to act to positively impact your future. You're not some helpless person being whisked down a flooded river, clinging to a piece of wood trying to keep your head above water. At least, I hope not, though at times life can certainly feel that way.

You're a person with a vision, with a plan, and with the drive and ambition to work those things to your benefit. You've got this. And if you've read this far, you're already well ahead of where you were when you started it.

Good job.

Keep going.

CHAPTER NINE

Philanthropy: Stepping In and Stepping Up

Why would you want personal success? To be comfortable, certainly. To enjoy a pleasant lifestyle, to support your family in their endeavors, to be able to look down the road at the unknown future and feel reasonably sure you've got it covered—these are all good reasons. Maybe happiness for you means collecting some vintage cars (that's my thing) or buying a place at the lake to spend time with your kids and grandkids. Once you've got all you need and then some, once

your goals are in the rearview, how will you choose to use what you've learned and earned to leave a meaningful legacy?

When I hit that point in my life, I began to think about all the different kinds of needs I saw in the communities where our offices are located. What could one guy do to help fill the gaps between what needed doing and what the local and state governments were actually getting done? I found inspiration in the life of a banker who lived in the Twin Cities back in the early twentieth century, a German immigrant named Otto Bremer. He started a bank, then during the Depression he saved a lot of small local banks, showing up with sacks full of cash when they were failing, ultimately owning stock in them all. He came close to failing himself, but his nerve never failed, and he wound up even richer than before once the Depression was over.

A success by any measure, Bremer looked around and asked himself what he could do to make his corner of the world a better place. He decided to start a foundation—the Bremer Foundation—and direct the profits of the Bremer bank holding company to support it. As of 2009, the foundation was donating $25 million a year, "Making grants to nonprofit and other qualified organizations working to improve lives in the Upper Midwest," in the categories of covering basic needs for those who were struggling, community asset building, health and well-being, and restorative and emergency services.

The Bremer Bank is still going strong, and so is the foundation. Otto Bremer will be remembered by many people not for his success as a banker or the risks he took during the Depression but by the legacy of good he left to carry on his name and help the people of the communities in which his banks are located. That's pretty cool.

When I first heard that story, it caught my attention. I had a good feeling about it. It inspired me to consider what our community needed. Looking around the communities where my offices are located through the lens of my years in real estate, I wondered, "Why are so many salvageable buildings being allowed to fall down, when so many people are homeless?" I thought about that, and about my area of expertise and how I'd started out in my twenties, buying busted-up houses and rehabbing them. We have a lot of people in need of housing, and that seemed like a natural fit since I knew how the process worked and brought some expertise to it.

And I know how important it is, especially for families with kids, to have a safe and livable place to call home. I know what it was like; when I grew up, if you lived in the butt end of Northeast, you were treated like a butt. There's discrimination based upon where you live and how you live. We're just trying to upgrade as many people as we can into a modest lifestyle—homes that are safe and clean and where everything works. We're not looking to do anything fancy, but it's amazing what a difference it can make in your quality of life if your plumbing, heat, and electricity work. And that's not the case with beat-up inner-city housing, generally.

That was the genesis of the Results Foundation. I donated the seed money to get it started, and now it's supported by RE/MAX Results. The foundation gets a portion of every transaction RE/MAX Results does, plus shares of profits from our mortgage and title companies and the holding company that owns a number of office buildings. Many of our sales executives also contribute a portion of their transactions. Gradually, we're putting all of my business assets into the foundation.

I've had the conversation with my kids: "Hey, good luck, you guys. You're not getting any of the business stuff, because I'm giving it to the foundation to help people," and they're okay with that. By the time I'm in the ground, the foundation will be a multimillion-dollar enterprise and able to help even more people. We do some other kinds of stuff too. We fund twelve students per year with scholarships to the University of Minnesota. But housing is our main focus and will continue to be because that's the business we're in, and it makes sense to go with your strengths.

We don't work with governmental agencies, but we *do* work with other nonprofits who help us to identify people in need of housing in the communities.

I see huge unmet needs in the communities around Minneapolis. It's a mess, and it's really troubling for somebody like me, who grew up and went to school there. It's a struggling community, but the people in charge don't seem to be able to move the needle on crime and property destruction or get the police department up to par. That's hard to do, because understandably people aren't lining up to become police officers there. I'm not pretending to have the solutions. I know that all we can do is take on one situation, one individual, one family, one house at a time. I can't solve all the problems, but I can help out families one at a time and have a positive impact on those individuals and the community. When you stabilize a single house on the street, it impacts all of the neighborhood.

WHEN YOU STABILIZE A SINGLE HOUSE ON THE STREET, IT IMPACTS ALL OF THE NEIGHBORHOOD.

Why have things gotten so bad for North Minneapolis? I don't know. I've heard it is blamed on real estate conglomerates whose owners are outside of the US and whose properties are allowed to fall apart because, why not? They don't live around here, and they don't see or care about the destruction of neighborhoods. Whatever's good for their bottom line is what their decisions are based on. It costs money to maintain and renovate a building, but these folks want to suck as much money out of these properties as they can, because they're only interested in profitability, not the community. To me, that's a dark hole. I'm not for that; that's not who I am or how I've led my life. I think it matters if you mow the lawn. I think it matters if you fix the garage up, because a home's appearance impacts the neighborhood. When the neighborhood is full of rat-trap houses, becoming more and more sketchy and less and less familial, you're raising a generation of kids who just don't care or even see why they should. They're seeing things from a different perspective, one that's relatively negative, and they don't have a sense of community. In their view, it's a stacked deck, and they can't win. Why should they care about the homes around them? Why not just burn them down if they feel like it? Same thing with housing projects; if you have no investment and no sense of ownership, why care about it?

When you help people into home ownership—people who otherwise wouldn't have that possibility—and you're pulling the neighborhood up by turning wrecks into nice homes, everyone wins.

The Cost of Failure? A Divided Nation

Here's the thing: if we can't get people invested in their communities, those communities are going to fail. But the failure starts with the institutions that aren't doing their jobs. We have schools that, for whatever reasons and despite teachers' best efforts, are turning out kids without the basic skills they need to work. They're too often functionally illiterate, unable to do simple math, unequipped to go on to higher education or to bring value to the work force. There are always kids who, because of higher-than-average intelligence or parents who push them to succeed, get out of that cycle of despair and failure and go on to become successful. But the vast majority of kids stuck in failing schools and without those resources have no hope for escape. I see stories every day of school or government officials dumbing down tests and expectations so that everyone graduates—with a worthless high school degree that is devalued because it no longer dependably indicates the student has any level of mastery at all. How is that fair to these kids? And how does that serve them? In my view it isn't, and it doesn't.

It's not just the kids who are failing; their parents are failing them when they let them run wild, skip school, or get involved in criminal activities. I was one of those kids myself, and I know that if my mother had been raising me on her own, there's no way in hell she could have kept me out of trouble. My father was a difficult guy, and we have a bad history, but to the extent that I was kept in line at home, he was the one drawing that line and holding me to it. He was an educated man, but we never had any rapport. We weren't able to connect. Is that his fault? I don't know. It's part mine, but I think it's part his too. I think he gave up on me when I was in and out of jail, because he wouldn't come and pick me up when I was released. That sent me a strong signal of how little he cared, which didn't exactly strengthen our relationship.

But what would I have done in his place, with a difficult kid on my hands and no communication skills? I was already chemically dependent, but the idea that I was a drug addict and an alcoholic at seventeen was incomprehensible to my parents. The prevailing attitude toward delinquents like me was, "Oh, they're just being kids," like addiction was some normal rite of passage. That's as bad as thinking that some degree of criminality is normal and acceptable for a teenager. If it is, it shouldn't be.

How Do We Teach a Work Ethic?

The only way I know is to teach by example. My dad worked his ass off and expected me to work my ass off. Somehow, that got through to me once I sobered up. He walked the walk—and set a pretty tough pace to follow.

Here's an example: He had throat cancer and had to have a tracheotomy. He got out of the hospital on a Saturday, then went to work on Monday. He couldn't talk; for a long time, the only way he could communicate was by writing notes. Eventually, he relearned how to talk, but in the meantime if he was trying to tell me to do something and I walked away, he'd grab me by the shirt and hold a note card up in front of my face. He did that to the people who worked for him too, because he had a job to do, and if that meant writing out a hundred note cards to give orders, that's what he'd do. That made an impression on me, as hard a case as I was. Despite the differences we had and despite how disconnected I was, I couldn't help but notice that my dad was a tough guy and wasn't afraid of much. Not many people could have gone right back to work the way he did after having that kind of a surgery. That's what I call modeling an impressive work ethic.

How Do We Give Kids Skin in the Game?

How do you give a kid a sense that their community is worthwhile and that they themselves are worthwhile members of society with the agency to improve things? Again, I think this should be the work of the institutions we fund with tax dollars. Every child who is able should be tasked with doing work in the community by the time they're in eighth grade if not earlier. They should work in the food pantries. They should be cooking for and serving dinner to the homeless at shelters or churches. They should be cleaning up their neighborhoods, block by block, picking up garbage or washing sidewalks.

When you get kids out into the real world doing positive things, it gives them a better perspective on life and what good they're capable of. Kids should be picking up garbage with freeway crews or in neighborhood parks, doing something to make the world a little better—and not just the kids who get in trouble, but every child. Get crews of kids together to clean up a neighbor's yard—that makes a huge difference to the person and to the looks of the neighborhood in general. It engenders pride for the kids—in a job well done, in visible success, in doing something generous. Those are good things, and they can change lives. Public schools should be assigning this work in the way that religious schools often do.

Clearly, there's more we could do to make ourselves feel like a community, especially since some of the nongovernmental institutions we used to depend on to create that sense of belonging don't have the reach or popularity that they did years ago. When I was growing up, the strongest institution in northeast Minneapolis was the Catholic Church. It gave people a reason to get together and a way to do outreach to needy parishioners. I don't see that happening as much anymore, as people have pulled away from organized religion. But they haven't put anything in its place.

I know that not everybody's on board with the Church, and certainly I never bought into the spiritual message, but I did like the camaraderie I found in Catholic schools. There was a teacher, Brother Mark, a Christian brother who I liked a lot and who taught my religion class. One day he asked me to stop by his room after school. When I got there, he said, "John, you don't believe any of this, do you?"

I said, "No, I'm sorry. I kind of don't get it. I just don't feel it. I don't think this is the real deal."

And he told me, "Well, you know, that's not wrong. You can believe whatever you want, but you still have to be a good person to feel good about yourself. So if you don't believe in the same things I do, I support you 100 percent, but you have to learn how to give back and be part of the community. That's got nothing to do with whether you believe in Jesus Christ or not. That just has the fact that you live in this world, and you have to participate in it." That's a pretty powerful thing to tell a tenth grader, and the message stuck with me all these years. I didn't always act on it. I did fall off the wagon a few times in terms of my behavior, but on the other hand, it did stick with me. Just because you don't go to church every Sunday, that has nothing to do with whether you're a good person or not. Your goodness is judged on how you treat other people and what you're doing in the community. That thought was probably the genesis of my foundation.

Addressing Homelessness

Something that doesn't get said often enough is that for people living on the streets, homelessness is often a choice. Clearly, that's not true for everyone, but for those who are choosing drugs or alcohol, it can be.

When I was a hippie hitchhiking around California, I would sleep anywhere. I could sometimes hide in a restroom down by the beach so I could sleep in there at night, but it was a choice. I was homeless, and I had no money. I went to the food pantry and the shelter to eat, but it was a choice. I didn't want to be back in Minneapolis working. I didn't want to try and start a new life in California. I wanted to be a bum. I can tell you from experience that there is a relatively high percentage of people who end up homeless either because of addiction or mental health. And that's a tough deal. Honestly, the only people I have empathy for are homeless women with children, and I believe we have to provide them with housing and support at any cost. But this guy standing on the corner, who's twenty-seven years old and could go down to the Salvation Army or wherever and say, "Clean me up. I want to get a job," is making a choice. And it's not good for him or the society he's living off of.

I used to spend some time down at the Salvation Army, and there was a guy there who I got to know who'd been homeless for twenty or thirty years and in and out of jail. First thing he'd do when he was released was go and get drunk again. He chose that lifestyle; he wanted to stay drunk and sleep under the bridge. It was a choice. Finally, something happened, and he realized that his life sucked, and that booze was the issue. He sobered up, and his job at the Salvation Army was to help other people who had sobered up to get an apartment and find a job. Remember, he'd been a bum and a lush for decades, but he cleaned up and reclaimed his life. It wasn't easy, and not everyone can do it, but he did it because he decided he wanted something better.

How do we fix this? If it's a mental health issue, there is medication available to treat it. But someone has to make sure that the person who needs the meds is getting them and taking them on schedule, and that's impossible to monitor if your patient is living under an overpass.

As someone who has anxiety and depression, I've been on medication for years. A few months ago, I asked my shrink, "So what happens if I quit taking my meds?"

"Try it and find out," he said.

Well, I did. And I did find out, and the cloud of depression reappeared in a relatively short period of time. I'd forgotten what that felt like and realized that there was no way and no reason to try to do without the drugs. It has nothing to do with whether I'm smart, dumb, or lazy. It has to do with my brain chemistry.

So how do you motivate people who aren't motivated to change their lives to get off the streets and become responsible citizens? Sobering up is the necessary first step. After that you can work on the things that are making you crazy. But I couldn't work on my depression when I was drunk. I needed sobriety, and then I needed to figure out what other things I wanted to do. That wasn't easy. It took me a long time to understand normalcy and the control I had over my own life and to acknowledge that I was the one deciding every morning whether I was going to be happy or not. I didn't believe that for a long, long time.

But I would have never had that revelation if I'd stayed drunk. And I might be the guy with his butt parked on the sidewalk, begging for change.

When it comes to our nation and our neighborhoods, we all have skin in the game. Let's use what we know and what we've accomplished to help end the cycle of poverty and solve the big problems, like homelessness and addiction, that are pulling us down.

Work on It

We may not all have the funds to found philanthropic organizations, but we all have the time to contribute in some way, even if that means giving up spare time to help them do the work. My employees are encouraged to do that in the neighborhoods where they work because I think we have to understand the problems at ground level if we're going to be good neighbors and good citizens.

THE PEOPLE WHO RISE ABOVE THE CROWD ARE THE ONES WHO PUT IN THE WORK TO MAKE THINGS BETTER. BE THAT PERSON, NO MATTER WHERE YOU ARE IN YOUR LIFE.

It's never too soon to think about the kind of legacy you're going to leave, whether you're already successful or just starting out in life. Pondering the impact for good that you can have as one person with agency in the world is empowering. Teaching your children the value of helping others by providing an example of volunteerism in action is the greatest gift you can give them and a valuable legacy in itself.

What are the issues where you live? From a distance they can seem so huge and intractable that it's tough to see what you as one person can do to help. But there are almost certainly good organizations already on the ground working on those problems, and those kinds of places always need good people who will step up and help out.

If you've never seen a homeless mom and kids as they toured their new rehabbed home with the volunteers that made it happen, you don't know how profoundly good it makes you feel to know you had a part in that. You've had an impact—not just on the mom but, generationally, on the kids. They'll learn from that example too, and maybe avoid the trap of despair that catches so many kids who live in poverty. Believe me, it's worth a couple of days off a month or more to help. Everyone complains about how things are. The people who rise above the crowd are the ones who put in the work to make things better.

Be that person, no matter where you are in your life.

To the Point

Did you know that there's fairly significant research showing that your life is enhanced in multiple ways by doing volunteer work? Giving doesn't only support the receiver but does a lot of good for the giver too.

How, you ask? Here's how:

1. When you're engaged in an act of giving—volunteering, working for a charity, extending a hand to someone who needs it—it actually releases the neurotransmitter and hormone dopamine into your brain, which gives you a rush of happiness and satisfaction and relieves stress.
2. Millennials like to feel they work for a company that does good in the world and are drawn to jobs that give them the

opportunity to engage in community service on some level. In 2015, the Deloitte Survey reported that six out of ten Millennials actually chose their jobs because they felt a sense of purpose there. That's a good reason to get your business involved in some kind of team-wide philanthropic effort, whether you're a team member or the owner, because good work environments are more likely to attract higher-level employees, and good people are hard to come by. Volunteering can provide great team-building time too, with a lot more meaningful interactions than the typical team exercise thing will.

3. If you're giving your volunteer hours in the community in which you live or the one in which you work, you're making your hometown and/or workplace a better place to live. A healthy community has engaged citizens.

4. It bears mentioning again that when you do philanthropic work, it is good for your kids, because you're modeling good citizenship in a manner that you'd want to see your kids copy. Getting the family involved, even if tangentially, makes it all that much more meaningful.

5. Not at the least, you meet really good people when you work with charitable organizations, and that's always a good thing. You learn more about the people who live in your community, and you'll probably make new friends because working together for a good cause is deeply satisfying.

AFTERWORD

About John

John Collopy is a speaker, coach, and philanthropist, usually found traveling between one of RE/MAX Results' forty-three offices throughout Minnesota and Wisconsin. John is available for speaking engagements, conferences, and interviews. His first book, *The Reward of Knowing*, is available on Amazon. To contact John or find out more about him, visit johncollopy.com. To learn more about the Results Foundation, visit resultsfoundation.net.

About RE/MAX Results

What's the secret sauce that's allowed RE/MAX Results to experience the exponential growth we've enjoyed, and what drives us forward? At RE/MAX Results the sales executives are the customers. The buyers and sellers pay the sales executives, and we work for them, not the other way around. We empower our sales executives by providing superior customer service to those buyers and sellers. It's a seemingly simple distinction that's had a profound impact on our success. To learn more, visit results.net.